RADIX READING for the TOEFL iBT®

BLACK LABEL

2

RADIX READING
FOR THE TOEFL iBT®:
BLACK LABEL 2

Series editor	Ji Hyun Kim
Project editors	Yuram Jo, Yeonsue Choi, Hyejin Kim
Contributing writers	Bryce Olk, Nathaniel Galletta, Tamar Harrington, Michael Ledezma, MyAn Le
Design	dots
Editorial designer	In-sun Lee
Photo Credits	www.shutterstock.com

www.neungyule.com

TABLE OF CONTENTS

INTRODUCTION

TOEFL®: Test of English as a Foreign Language

The TOEFL is a standardized test developed to assess English language proficiency in an academic setting. By achieving a high score on the TOEFL, you will demonstrate that your skills in English qualify you for admission to a college or university where English is used as the language of instruction. Academic institutions around the world will look at your performance on the TOEFL, so whether you are hoping to study in North America, Australia, Europe, or Asia, this test is the key to your future educational career.

TOEFL Today: TOEFL iBT

The TOEFL Internet-based test (iBT) is the version currently administered in secure testing centers worldwide. It tests reading, listening and writing proficiency, and speaking abilities.

Getting to Know the TOEFL iBT: Important Points

≫ The test is divided into four sections: Reading, Listening, Speaking, and Writing. These are the skills that are essential for proficiency in any language.

≫ As well as measuring the individual skills listed above, some portions of the test require you to apply various combinations of skills in order to complete a task. Examples of such integrated tasks include:
  - listening to a passage and speaking in response to a question on the passage
  - reading a passage, listening to a second passage, and then speaking in response to a question on the two passages
  - reading a passage, listening to a second passage, and then writing a response to a question on the two passages

≫ In each section of the test, a tool bar is displayed on the computer screen. It lists the section and question number you are currently working on, the amount of time remaining, and has help, navigational, and volume buttons. The function buttons may differ slightly from one section to the next.

≫ In the Speaking section of the test, you will be required to speak your responses into a microphone. Your input will be digitally recorded and evaluated by ETS's trained scorers.

≫ In the Writing section of the test, you will be required to type your responses.

≫ There is no section dedicated to grammar, but your grammar skills will be tested indirectly throughout the test, especially in the Speaking and Writing sections.

≫ You will be allowed to take notes during all portions of the test, and you will likely find these notes very helpful when answering the questions.

≫ You can view your scores in your ETS account approximately 6 days after your test date. You'll receive an email when your scores are available, and you can access your account online or via the official TOEFL® app.

Getting to Know the TOEFL iBT: Test Format

You will take all four sections of the test (Reading, Listening, Speaking, and Writing) on the same day. The duration of the entire test is about four hours.

Test Section	Description of Tasks	Timing
Reading	3–4 passages, each approximately 700 words 10 questions on each passage	54–72 minutes

Listening	• 3–4 lectures, each 3–5 minutes long
	  6 questions per lecture
	• 2–3 conversations, each around 3 minutes long
	  5 questions per conversation
		41–57 minutes

	BREAK	10 minutes
Speaking	4 tasks • 1 independent task – speak about personal knowledge and experience • 3 integrated tasks – read-listen-speak / listen-speak	17 minutes
Writing	2 tasks • 1 independent task – write about personal knowledge and experience • 1 integrated task – read-listen-write	50 minutes

Score Scales

You will receive a score between 0 and 30 for each section of the test. Your total score is the sum of these four scores and will be between 0 and 120.

Registering for the TOEFL iBT

The most convenient way to register to take the TOEFL iBT is online by visiting the "Register for the TOFEL® Test" section of the TOEFL website (www.ets.org/toefl). Here, you can check current listings of testing centers and schedules. It is also possible to register for the test by phone and by mail. For more information, consult the TOEFL iBT Bulletin, which can be downloaded or ordered from the TOEFL website. It is free and features important information regarding the registration process.

GUIDE TO READING

Success in an English-speaking academic environment demands high-level reading comprehension skills. The Reading Section of the TOEFL iBT requires you to understand and analyze texts similar to those used at academic institutions across North America and throughout the world. Questions in the Reading Section are designed to test:

1. Your ability to identify important details in an academic text, including the meaning of selected vocabulary terms, the noun referred to by a pronoun or other reference word, the fundamental meaning of complex sentences, and facts relevant to the main idea of a passage
2. Your ability to draw inferences regarding implied information, the intent or attitude of the author, and the relationship between ideas in different parts of a passage
3. Your understanding of the organization of a passage, including how major points relate to the main idea and how an individual sentence is connected to the sentences around it

Reading Section Content: Types of Passages

The material you will see in the Reading Section will include texts typical of college-level textbooks used in introductory courses. Topics covered are quite varied, but no prior knowledge or expertise is required to understand the material. You will be able to answer all the questions using only the information contained in the passages.

Passages that appear in the Reading Section fall into three categories:
1. Exposition: a text that is factual in nature, with the primary purpose of providing an explanation of a topic
2. Argumentation: a text offering a specific point of view on an issue, with the primary purpose of persuading readers through the presentation of evidence
3. Historical/Biographical: a text providing an account of a historical event or the life of a notable individual

Types of Questions

The questions found in the Reading Section can be divided into 9 categories.

Question Type	Testing Point
Vocabulary	The meaning of a highlighted word or phrase, determined by context
Reference	The noun referred to by a pronoun or other reference word
Fact & Negative Fact	Important details presented in the passage / An idea that is not factually correct according to the passage
Sentence Simplification	The fundamental meaning of a complex sentence
Inference	Information that is implied, rather than directly stated, in the passage
Rhetorical Purpose	The author's purpose for including certain information in the passage
Insertion	The logical position at which to insert a given sentence into the passage
Prose Summary	The completion of a summary of the passage by choosing the most relevant and important information
Schematic Table	The correct categorization of information from the passage

Important Points to Keep in Mind

≫ Questions appear only after you have scrolled to the end of the passage. After they appear, you will be able to see the passage on the right side of the screen as you answer the questions on the left.

≫ Certain words and phrases in the passages will have a "Glossary Feature" associated with them. Clicking on these underlined words and phrases will produce a box containing a definition or explanation.

≫ The TOEFL iBT Reading section includes question types that are different from the traditional multiple-choice format, including Insertion, Prose Summary, and Schematic Table questions.

Tactics for the TOEFL iBT Reading Section

To strengthen your reading skills before taking the TOEFL iBT, it is essential to expose yourself frequently to written English. Focus should be placed on texts that are academic in nature, but it is also important to seek out material from diverse sources that cover a variety of topics. The Internet is an excellent source of free articles on an array of subjects, particularly social and physical sciences, arts and business. Textbooks and journals are also helpful resources.

Other recommended activities to pursue before taking the test include:

- practicing scanning of passages to identify important details
- familiarizing yourself with the standard organizational formats of academic texts

During the test, remember to:

- write down brief notes about the organization, main idea, and key details of the passage
- pay attention to the flow of ideas in the passage and how they relate to one another
- think about the author's motivation for writing the passage and presenting certain information
- determine the key words of answer choices and locate them in the passage to help you identify the correct answer

HOW TO USE THIS BOOK

This book gives you instruction, practice, and strategies for performing well on the TOEFL iBT Reading Section. It will familiarize you with the appearance and format of the TOEFL iBT and help you prepare for the TOEFL test efficiently.

Each unit in the book corresponds to one of the nine question types in the Reading Section. Each unit consists of the following:

- An **Introduction** that provides basic information about and strategies for the question type
- A **Vocabulary Preview** and **Review** that offer various activities to help you increase vocabulary knowledge and retention
- **Basic Drills** that offer short passages and give examples of the question type being covered
- **Reading Practice** that involves longer passages with 1–3 questions so that you can master skills for the question type
- **iBT Practice** that includes long passages with 7 questions so that you can experience and practice the various question types
- An **Actual Practice Test** that enables you to measure your development by providing long passages with 10 questions

At the end of the book, you will find a **Practice TOEFL iBT Reading Section** that provides you with sample test questions to give you an estimate of how you would perform on the actual TOEFL test.

PART A

Identifying Details

UNIT

01

Vocabulary

Vocabulary Preview

A **Choose the word that best matches each definition.**

> Ⓐ shovel   Ⓑ maturation   Ⓒ pit
>
> Ⓓ shed   Ⓔ eruption   Ⓕ reserve

1. to keep a thing for a specific purpose: _____
2. to release something from a body of a plant or an animal in a natural way: _____
3. an outburst that is sudden and sometimes violent: _____
4. to remove or dig material with a broad-blade tool: _____
5. the process of a person's physical growth and mental development: _____

B **Choose the best synonym for each list of words.**

> Ⓐ dense   Ⓑ surplus   Ⓒ sensory   Ⓓ feast
>
> Ⓔ heir   Ⓕ bountiful   Ⓖ explore

1. ample   plentiful   abundant   : _____
2. dinner party   banquet   fiesta   : _____
3. excess   extra   spare   : _____
4. investigate   search   examine   : _____
5. concentrated   thick   compressed   : _____
6. successor   inheritor   descendant   : _____

C **Choose the right meaning for each highlighted word.**

1. Many sociologists study the way immigrants assimilate into their new environment.
   - Ⓐ to conform or adjust to something
   - Ⓑ to grow more comfortable

2. One basic skill that our laboratory assistant taught us was how to dilute a solution.
   - Ⓐ to make something more clear
   - Ⓑ to weaken the concentration of a liquid

3. Tim was promoted for doing so much extra work for the company.
   - Ⓐ to receive a higher position with more pay
   - Ⓑ to get recognition from higher-ranked officials

4. The relationship of one's self to others is often related to how egocentric one is.
   - Ⓐ generous in sharing one's things and time
   - Ⓑ limited in attitude by centering on one's self

01 Vocabulary

Introduction

- Vocabulary questions require you to find the meaning of the given word or phrase as it is used within the context of the passage.

- Tested words or phrases are highlighted within the passage.

- 1 to 3 vocabulary questions are given for each passage.

Question Types

- The word [____] in the passage is closest in meaning to

- The phrase [____] in the passage is closest in meaning to

Strategy

1. A word can have more than one meaning. Even if you think you know the word, take care to focus on how it is used within the given context.

2. If you don't know the given vocabulary word, use clues provided by the context to figure out its meaning. They may include the following forms:
   ① Examples: such as, for example, for instance, colon (:)
   ② Similar expressions or synonyms
   ③ Additional explanation: relative clauses, adverbial clauses, participles
   ④ Equivalence: dash (—), comma (,)
   ⑤ Sentence structure that shows comparison, contrast, cause and effect, etc.

3. Finding the answer can be helped by understanding the general flow of the passage or having some background knowledge of the topic.

4. Substitute each answer choice into the passage and then decide whether the answer choice has the same contextual meaning as the original word in the passage.

Basic Drills

Tropical rain forests are ideal breeding grounds for bacteria and other microorganisms because of the constant warmth and abundant moisture in tropical environments. Due to the fact that these organisms remain active all year, they rapidly break down matter on the forest floor. In other biomes, for instance, forests where trees shed their leaves seasonally, the decomposition of fallen leaves adds nutrients to the soil. However, in tropical rain forests, plants grow so quickly that they soon consume the nutrients made available by such fallen leaves. As a consequence, the majority of nutrients are passed on to the trees and other plants of the rain forest rather than to the soil, which results in the soil becoming infertile.

1   The word decomposition in the passage is closest in meaning to
    (A) movement   (B) discoloration   (C) decay   (D) deposit

2   The word consume in the passage is closest in meaning to
    (A) exclude   (B) diminish   (C) absorb   (D) refine

3   The word infertile in the passage is closest in meaning to
    (A) plentiful   (B) barren   (C) dense   (D) stable

Desertification occurs when dry regions bordering deserts suffer persistent land degradation because of a reduction in biological productivity and an exhaustion of soil nutrients. An obvious explanation for desertification is climate change, but unsustainable agricultural practices by humans, such as poor irrigation, overgrazing, and deforestation, also add to the problem. Desertification has serious consequences because it negatively affects the livelihoods of millions of people who need dryland ecosystems to survive. The decrease in plant cover that goes along with desertification results in an increase in soil erosion by wind and water. This is followed by loss of the land's ability to sustain crops, animals, or human activity by depleting important soil nutrients required for the production of food. Furthermore, the frequency of sand and dust storms is increased, and these dust storms can make their way to cities around the world. This in turn exacerbates health problems, including eye infections, respiratory illnesses, and allergies.

4   The word persistent in the passage is closest in meaning to
    (A) lengthy   (B) continual   (C) extreme   (D) dangerous

5   The word depleting in the passage is closest in meaning to
    (A) affecting   (B) building   (C) including   (D) lessening

6   The word exacerbates in the passage is closest in meaning to
    (A) worsens   (B) discovers   (C) causes   (D) cures

A potlatch was a special cultural practice among certain American Indian tribes on the Pacific Northwest coast of the United States and the Canadian province of British Columbia. Potlatches were held when a family had a special event to celebrate, such as births, rites of passages, weddings, funerals, and honoring of the deceased. Hosts would invite members of their own tribe, as well as neighboring tribes, to come to a feast. 5

Potlatches took the form of a ceremonial meal traditionally featuring seal meat or salmon. To exhibit generosity, good hosts were expected to offer plentiful food. During potlatches, hosts showed their wealth and prominence by giving guests resources such as canoes, bowls and spoons, carvings, tools, and blankets gathered for these events. The value of a gift was determined by a guest's social rank. The most valuable gifts were reserved for chiefs and 10 nobles, while commoners received items of lesser value. When potlatches were finished, it was expected that wealthier guests would reciprocate in turn. Thus, even if hosts totally impoverished themselves, they could expect wealth to be returned to them when they attended subsequent potlatches as guests. As the nature of gifting varied through time, some potlatches became highly competitive, with hosts bankrupting themselves to outdo others. 15

The potlatch enhanced the host's reputation and validated his social rank – the larger the ceremony, the greater this effect was. The potlatch also served to redistribute wealth among villages, give away surplus product, and connect villages to one another socially. Furthermore, potlatches were the place in which ownership of economic and ceremonial privileges was asserted, displayed, and formally transferred to heirs. 20

1 The word prominence in the passage is closest in meaning to

- Ⓐ appreciation
- Ⓑ standing
- Ⓒ tolerance
- Ⓓ permanence

2 The word reciprocate in the passage is closest in meaning to

- Ⓐ collaborate
- Ⓑ attend
- Ⓒ reply
- Ⓓ repay

3 The word validated in the passage is closest in meaning to

- Ⓐ utilized
- Ⓑ confirmed
- Ⓒ confined
- Ⓓ judged

Extra Question

According to the passage, a potlatch served an important economic role by

- Ⓐ saving surplus product for times of hardship
- Ⓑ encouraging competition among wealthy guests
- Ⓒ leading to the destruction of surplus wealth
- Ⓓ reorganizing wealth and redistributing surplus product

Organization

- Potlatch — a cultural practice in American Indian tribes
- Practice of giving gifts
  - showing the host's _____ and prominence
  - value of gift determined by a guest's _____ _____
  - wealthy guests' reciprocating in turn
  - competitive nature
- Social functions of potlatches — connection with _____, social rank, and redistribution of wealth

"Fresco" means "fresh" in Italian, which is an appropriate name for this form of mural painting in which paint is applied to fresh, wet plaster. The paint is made by diluting colored dyes with water. Once the plaster has been smoothed onto a surface (usually a wall), an outline of the picture is drawn and finally the paint is applied. As the paint forms a chemical bond with the plaster, the fresco becomes insoluble and will stay intact for thousands of years.　　　　　5

Around 400 BC, fresco painting became popular in ancient Rome, especially as a means of decoration. Frescoes were the preferred method of interior decoration for the wealthy. Artists created sophisticated and elaborate frescoes that were used for both important public buildings and the homes of Rome's elite. Pompeii, the city in the Roman Empire, which was preserved after the eruption of the volcano Vesuvius in 79 AD, is a treasure chest of perfectly preserved　10 frescoes. Houses in this city were relatively simple. Their interiors were very basic and small, with only the necessary items of furniture. Fresco paintings became a popular way of making these houses more aesthetically pleasing by featuring fresco paintings of figures, landscapes, and garlands on the walls. In addition to adding much needed beauty and color to a room, frescoes also served to give the illusion that the room was bigger than it actually was. This effect was given　15 by the broadened horizons of the paintings. Paintings for this purpose depicted rustic country landscapes, panoramic ocean views, or bountiful gardens. Among the most pleasing aspects of these wall paintings were the gardens populated with birds and flowers that bring the outside inside.

Glossary

plaster: a substance that is used to cover walls in order to give a smooth surface

1 The word intact in the passage is closest in meaning to

(A) distant

(B) undamaged

(C) glossy

(D) underrated

2 The word aesthetically in the passage is closest in meaning to

(A) obviously

(B) essentially

(C) technically

(D) artistically

3 The word rustic in the passage is closest in meaning to

(A) peaceful

(B) rural

(C) old-fashioned

(D) simple

Extra Question

According to paragraph 1, all of the following are mentioned about frescoes EXCEPT

(A) the origin of their name

(B) the effect of paint on frescoes

(C) the types of dyes used

(D) the method of painting

Summary

Fresco is the name given to a painting on wet _____ wall. After plaster is smoothed onto a surface, an outline is drawn and then paint is applied. Frescoes became popular around 400 BC in ancient _____, where they were used for _____ _____ by wealthy Romans. Frescoes became a popular way of making _____ look more pleasing to the eye by depicting colorful landscapes with flowers and birds. This led to the illusion that rooms were _____ than they actually were.

● iBT Practice 01

TOEFL Reading

The Life and Work of Frederick W. Taylor

Frederick Winslow Taylor, the father of scientific management, was born in 1856 to a wealthy <u>Quaker</u> family in the American city of Philadelphia. He served his apprenticeship as a patternmaker, acquiring shop-floor experience in 1874, and obtained a degree in mechanical engineering at the Stevens Institute of Technology while holding a full-time job. Following his apprenticeship, Taylor worked at the Midvale Steel Company, where he started as a laborer but 5 within six years was promoted to the role of research director, and then chief engineer.

Upon observing gross inefficiencies during his contact with steel workers early in his career, Taylor became interested in improving worker productivity. He thought that through planning even the most basic, mindless tasks could be carried out in a way to dramatically increase productivity. Taylor performed experiments that he labeled "time studies" to scientifically determine the best 10 way to perform a job. In these studies, a stopwatch was used to time a worker's sequence of motions, with the aim of determining the one best way to perform a job.

➡ Taylor put his ideas into practice in various settings. He believed the key to productivity was finding the right challenge for each person, so he used time studies to set daily production quotas. The idea was to give incentives to those workers who reached their daily quotas and 15 lower pay to those who did not. By way of his new wage system and time studies, Taylor doubled the productivity of the Midvale Steel Company.

Another famous example of his time studies was his groundbreaking work on "shoveling." He found the optimal weight of a shovel was 21 pounds and proceeded to design shovels that would hold 21 pounds of whatever substance was being shoveled. The use of optimal shovels allowed 20 a reduction in the workforce at Bethlehem Steel Company from 500 to 140 and achieved a 300 to 400% increase in productivity.

Taylor was the first person to present a scientific and systematic study of interactions among job requirements, tools, methods, and human skill to improve both output and work life in factories. With his scientific management he improved productivity and had a substantial 25 impact on industry. Despite his many striking achievements, his critics felt that his approach to work increased the monotony of work and dehumanized workers. They also thought scientific management ignored the psychological needs and capabilities of workers.

Glossary

Quaker: a religious community well-known for opposition to war

1. Which of the sentences below best expresses the essential information in the highlighted sentence in the passage? *Incorrect* choices change the meaning in important ways or leave out essential information.
   - (A) Taylor stated that basic tasks were easier to plan more efficiently.
   - (B) Taylor theorized that heightened productivity resulted in better planning.
   - (C) Taylor suggested that the only way to increase productivity was to plan properly.
   - (D) Taylor believed that productivity in any discipline could be enhanced by planning.

2. Why does the author mention daily production quotas?
   - (A) To show the shortcomings of his scientific method
   - (B) To contrast his new wage system with the old one
   - (C) To give an example of his successful application of time studies
   - (D) To show his success in establishing goals for production

3. What can be inferred from paragraph 3 about Taylor's view of the relationship between workers and wages?
   - (A) They should be paid more if they are producing more.
   - (B) They should be paid based on the hours that they work.
   - (C) They should be paid more so as to work harder.
   - (D) They should be paid according to their experience.

   Paragraph 3 is marked with an arrow [➡].

4. The word striking in the passage is closest in meaning to
   - (A) impressive   (B) helpful   (C) profound   (D) available

5. The word monotony in the passage is closest in meaning to
   - (A) efficiency   (B) uncertainty   (C) boredom   (D) intensity

6. All of the following are mentioned in the passage as a way of improving productivity EXCEPT

   (A) appropriate wage systems

   (B) efficient employment of tools

   (C) matching workers to the right challenges

   (D) providing employees with updated equipment

7. **Directions:** An introductory sentence for a brief summary of the passage is provided below. Complete the summary by selecting the THREE answer choices that express the most important ideas in the passage. Some sentences do not belong in the summary because they express ideas that are not presented in the passage or are minor ideas in the passage. ***This question is worth 2 points.***

> Frederick W. Taylor used his knowledge of scientific management to improve the performance of American workers.
>
> -
> -
> -

Answer Choices

   (A) Taylor worked as a laborer at Midvale Steel Company before rising to the position of chief engineer.

   (B) Critics claim that Taylor's approach led to monotony among workers and failed to address their needs.

   (C) He performed a series of time studies to find out the one best way to carry out a particular task.

   (D) Taylor's new wage system and the use of optimal tools brought about an improvement in productivity.

   (E) Through his systematic approach, Taylor succeeded in increasing output and profoundly influencing the industry.

   (F) Taylor introduced more hi-tech shovels for the employees of Bethlehem Steel Company.

Drag your answer choices to the spaces where they belong. To remove an answer choice, click on it. To review the passage, click on **View Text**.

● iBT Practice 02

PART A

UNIT 01 VOCABULARY

Granite

One of the most common types of intrusive igneous rock is granite. It is formed when molten rock, which is known as magma, cools and hardens deep within the earth's crust. Because this cooling occurs slowly in subterranean environments that are subject to extreme pressure, the resulting rock is exceptionally dense and hard. These same factors also cause granite to be coarse-grained, the characteristic from which its name is derived: *granum* being the Latin word ₅ for "grain." Granite can be found in abundance at the core of mountain ranges in every continent across the world, where it is excavated from the earth in large slabs from open pits known as quarries.

→ There are many different types of granite, each featuring its own unique combination of minerals. The vast majority of these minerals can be categorized into three distinct groups. The ₁₀ most predominant group is feldspar, which generally accounts for more than half of granite's total composition. The next most common group is quartz, which is the hardest component to be found in granite. Of the remaining components, the bulk is made up of a group of dark-colored minerals such as mica. Because granite is coarse-grained, each of these individual components is clearly visible to the naked eye. It is the relative concentration of these minerals that dictates the color of ₁₅ the granite, which most commonly varies in shades from grayish-white to pink, although bolder colors such as red and black are not unknown.

Some of granite's most basic characteristics are what make it so appealing to the construction industry. It retains its color and texture over time, and because it is so hard, it resists scratching, chipping, and other forms of damage. In fact, the only natural material that is harder than granite ₂₀ is diamond. And because it is widespread and plentiful, granite is considerably less expensive than comparable materials like marble. Due to its durability, granite has been historically favored for use in building structures that are exposed to the elements, such as monuments, and in situations where it will experience extensive wear and tear, as in paving material for floors, steps, and public plazas. More recently, modern residential architects and designers have popularized ₂₅ granite as a practical and attractive material for kitchen countertops.

Glossary

the elements: the weather, especially violent or severe weather

1. The word subterranean in the passage is closest in meaning to

    (A) unique   (B) rough   (C) darkened   (D) underground

2. The word excavated in the passage is closest in meaning to

    (A) observed   (B) shaped   (C) mined   (D) kept

3. According to paragraph 2, the three types of minerals that usually make up granite are

    (A) similar in hardness   (B) all visible to the naked eye
    (C) most commonly dark in color   (D) dominated by minerals in the quartz category
    Paragraph 2 is marked with an arrow [➡].

4. Why does the author mention diamond?

    (A) To demonstrate the hardness of granite
    (B) To identify a major component of granite
    (C) To compare its value to that of granite
    (D) To describe the appearance of granite

5. Which of the sentences below best expresses the essential information in the highlighted
    sentence in the passage? *Incorrect* choices change the meaning in important ways or leave out
    essential information.

    (A) Many monuments and other public structures throughout the world were made of strong
        rock such as granite.
    (B) Granite is often used in circumstances where its durability helps it resist stronger than usual
        forces of wear and tear.
    (C) Outdoor monuments, floors, steps, and public plazas are all types of projects for which
        granite is specially suited.
    (D) One reason why construction with granite is so favorable is that the stone is able to last a
        long time.

6. All of the following are mentioned in the passage as characteristics of granite EXCEPT

- Ⓐ variation in color
- Ⓑ a high frequency of formation worldwide
- Ⓒ resistance to damage from exposure
- Ⓓ a smooth texture that is suitable for interior surfaces

7. **Directions:** An introductory sentence for a brief summary of the passage is provided below. Complete the summary by selecting the THREE answer choices that express the most important ideas in the passage. Some sentences do not belong in the summary because they express ideas that are not presented in the passage or are minor ideas in the passage. ***This question is worth 2 points.***

> Granite is a coarse-grained stone that can be found in many parts of the world and has been used frequently by humans.
>
> •
>
> •
>
> •

Answer Choices

- Ⓐ The low cost and durability of granite have made it popular in construction projects, from public monuments to kitchen countertops.
- Ⓑ Granite's name comes from a Latin word meaning "grain," referring to one of the rock's most notable features.
- Ⓒ The color of granite is determined by the relative concentration of its mineral components.
- Ⓓ Most granite comprises minerals from the feldspar, quartz, and mica families, each with a different appearance.
- Ⓔ Worldwide, granite has been used almost as often as marble when a strong stone material is needed.
- Ⓕ The extreme conditions under which granite forms are what give it its hardness and other special characteristics.

Drag your answer choices to the spaces where they belong. To remove an answer choice, click on it. To review the passage, click on **View Text**.

PART A

UNIT 01 VOCABULARY

Actual **Practice Test**

Piaget's Theory of Cognitive Development

→ According to child psychologist Jean Piaget, the mind assimilates new information by first attempting to incorporate it into one's existing view of the world. Sometimes, new information is incompatible with a person's established worldview. When this happens, it is necessary to analyze and modify thinking patterns in order to integrate the new information. In his work with children, Piaget observed that they think differently as they grow. He therefore concluded that a person's ability to process new information increases with maturation. Piaget believed that this cognitive development occurs universally among children and that it progresses through four stages. ⁵

→ From birth until about the age of two, children experience the sensorimotor stage. The name of this stage derives from the fact that information is gained through sensory perceptions and motor activities. Actions like seeing, touching, or sucking enable children in the sensorimotor ¹⁰ stage of development to explore their surroundings and learn about themselves. Their knowledge about their environment is gathered solely through physical interactions with it. Therefore, children's understanding of the world at this stage is narrow. Nonetheless, children in the sensorimotor stage make many important discoveries. Particularly significant is the discovery that they are separate from their environment. They realize that their surroundings are not extensions ¹⁵ of themselves. In addition, children in this stage become aware that objects continue to exist even when they are out of sight.

→ The preoperational stage occurs next, when children are between two and seven years old. ■ During this stage of cognitive development, children learn to use symbols to represent objects, and they become proficient in language. ■ They also learn how to classify objects ²⁰ according to a single characteristic such as size or shape. ■ Another characteristic of children at this stage of cognitive development is egocentric behavior. ■ This is caused by their inability to understand any perspective but their own.

As children acquire life experience, they become capable of reasoning in more sophisticated ways. Between the ages of seven and eleven, they enter the third stage of cognitive development, ²⁵ the concrete operational stage. At this stage, they begin to think more logically and can solve abstract problems. Along with these achievements comes a decrease in the egocentrism characteristic of the preoperational stage. In addition, children in this stage can classify objects according to several features. In the previous stage of development, they were only able to group objects together according to a single feature. ³⁰

→ The fourth stage of cognitive development is the formal operational stage. It begins when children are between eleven and fifteen and represents the ultimate stage of cognitive development. Adolescents in this stage of development are able to skillfully represent abstract concepts using symbols. Piaget pointed out, however, that some people never reach the formal

operational stage. Those who do have the ability to reason hypothetically and deductively. 35

➡ Piaget's theory of cognitive development has been very influential since the time of its proposal in 1969. However, not everyone is in agreement about exactly how children cognitively develop. Some psychologists wonder whether cognitive development can really be divided into four distinct stages. In spite of this, Piaget has had a significant impact on modern psychology and children's education. 40

1. The word integrate in the passage is closest in meaning to
   Ⓐ include
   Ⓑ edit
   Ⓒ repeat
   Ⓓ remember

2. In paragraph 1, the author introduces Piaget's theory of cognitive development by
   Ⓐ mentioning the work of psychologists who preceded Piaget
   Ⓑ describing Piaget's belief about how the mind deals with new information
   Ⓒ giving an example of how children act in each stage of cognitive development
   Ⓓ indicating that children who are the same age think in different ways
   Paragraph 1 is marked with an arrow [➡].

3. The word they in the passage refers to
   Ⓐ surroundings
   Ⓑ extensions
   Ⓒ children
   Ⓓ objects

4. According to paragraph 2, which of the following is a characteristic of children in the sensorimotor stage of development?
   Ⓐ They are able to use language to express their emotions.
   Ⓑ They do not have the ability to move themselves around.
   Ⓒ They realize they are separate from their surroundings.
   Ⓓ They have the ability to sort objects by shape.
   Paragraph 2 is marked with an arrow [➡].

5. The word proficient in the passage is closest in meaning to
   Ⓐ motivated
   Ⓑ competent
   Ⓒ remarkable
   Ⓓ understandable

6. Based on information in paragraph 3, what can be inferred about children in the preoperational stage?

    Ⓐ They can use tools to achieve their goals.

    Ⓑ They are likely to arrange objects from the smallest to the largest.

    Ⓒ They understand relationships between cause and effect.

    Ⓓ They have a tendency to personify objects around them.

    Paragraph 3 is marked with an arrow [➡].

7. According to paragraph 5, all of the following are true about the fourth stage EXCEPT

    Ⓐ people who reach it can reason hypothetically

    Ⓑ all 13-year-old children belong to this stage

    Ⓒ it represents cognition in its final form

    Ⓓ a child in this stage uses symbols related to abstract concepts

    Paragraph 5 is marked with an arrow [➡].

8. According to paragraph 6, what aspect of Piaget's theory has been criticized?

    Ⓐ The age at which the preoperational stage begins

    Ⓑ The assertion that egocentrism is universal

    Ⓒ The suggestion that cognitive development begins at birth

    Ⓓ The division of cognitive development into four stages

    Paragraph 6 is marked with an arrow [➡].

9. Look at the four squares [■] that indicate where the following sentence could be added to the passage.

    Such behavior is manifested in children's presumption that everyone else knows and sees the same things they do.

Where would the sentence best fit?

    Click on a square [■] to add the sentence to the passage.

10. **Directions:** An introductory sentence for a brief summary of the passage is provided below. Complete the summary by selecting the THREE answer choices that express the most important ideas in the passage. Some sentences do not belong in the summary because they express ideas that are not presented in the passage or are minor ideas in the passage. ***This question is worth 2 points.***

> Piaget's 1969 theory of cognitive development proposed that children think differently as they get older.
>
> •
>
> •
>
> •

Answer Choices

Ⓐ Piaget's theory has received both criticism and praise and has become quite influential in the fields of education and psychology.

Ⓑ There are times when new information encountered by a person is incompatible with existing ideas about how the world works.

Ⓒ The sensorimotor stage of cognitive development is one of four stages that Piaget suggested children progress through as they age.

Ⓓ Some people do not experience all four stages of cognitive development and may skip over the concrete operational stage.

Ⓔ Fundamental to Piaget's theory of cognitive development is the belief that people become better at assimilating new information as they mature.

Ⓕ Children's cognitive abilities become more sophisticated as they advance through the four stages of development.

Drag your answer choices to the spaces where they belong. To remove an answer choice, click on it. To review the passage, click on **View Text**.

Organization

Piaget's Theory of Cognitive Development

Introduction

Piaget's theory about the universal cognitive development of children

Sensorimotor stage

- from birth to about two years old
- Information is gained through _____ _____ and motor activities.
- Children discover that
  - they are separate from their _____.
  - objects continue to exist even when they are out of sight.

Preoperational stage

- from two to seven years old
- Children learn to use _____ / become _____ in language / classify objects according to a single characteristic.
- Children only understand their own _____.

Concrete operational stage

- from seven to eleven years old
- Children are able to think logically / solve _____ problems / classify objects according to _____ _____.
- Egocentric behavior is decreased.

Formal operational stage

- from eleven to fifteen years old
- Adolescents are able to represent _____ _____ using symbols.

Conclusion

Piaget's theory has had a significant impact on _____ _____ and children's _____.

Vocabulary Review

A   **Fill in the blanks with the best answer. Change the form if necessary.**

retain	diminish	manifest	carving	feature	gross

1. The truth will _____ itself through the eyewitness's statement as well as DNA testing.
2. Weather and season can naturally _____ the amount of light inside the beach house.
3. One great _____ about this magazine is its humorous essays on subjects that would otherwise be dry.
4. The children are not expected to _____ their mother tongue after they are adopted by German parents.
5. The company decided to dismiss the employee after he made such a(n) _____ error.

B   **Choose the word that is closest in meaning to each highlighted word.**

1. Mr. Brown transferred the ownership of his house to his sister.
   - Ⓐ guided
   - Ⓑ showed
   - Ⓒ promised
   - Ⓓ gave

2. They collaborated in writing a number of books and articles for thirty years.
   - Ⓐ competed
   - Ⓑ engaged
   - Ⓒ cooperated
   - Ⓓ argued

3. Some say that manipulation of the natural voice dehumanizes the art of music.
   - Ⓐ evaluates
   - Ⓑ complicates
   - Ⓒ mechanizes
   - Ⓓ revolutionizes

4. The two atoms are chemically combined by a mechanism called a chemical bond.
   - Ⓐ link
   - Ⓑ reaction
   - Ⓒ group
   - Ⓓ effect

5. Making conclusions based on presumptions can have very scary consequences.
   - Ⓐ researches
   - Ⓑ guesses
   - Ⓒ attempts
   - Ⓓ theories

6. He decided to change his job because he became tired of such mindless work.
   - Ⓐ tedious
   - Ⓑ terrible
   - Ⓒ complicated
   - Ⓓ planned

7. People living in slums have become even more impoverished as government spending has mainly gone into funding the war.
   - Ⓐ unhappy
   - Ⓑ poor
   - Ⓒ weak
   - Ⓓ discouraged

C   **Choose the correct word in each sentence.**

1. TV programs that target teenagers effectively (polarize, popularize) fashion and speech style.
2. Artists often (personify, purify) plants, animals, and weather among other natural elements.
3. It was the opinion of the cooking contest judge that the dish had a blend of (incompatible, incompetent) flavors.

UNIT

02

Reference

Vocabulary Preview

A Choose the word that best matches each definition.

Ⓐ aftermath	Ⓑ reflect	Ⓒ overpower
Ⓓ expel	Ⓔ famine	Ⓕ synthesize

1. to force to leave: _____
2. to show or reveal something: _____
3. result or consequence of an unpleasant incident: _____
4. to use force that is far stronger than or superior to others: _____
5. to produce something through a chemical reaction: _____

B Choose the best synonym for each list of words.

Ⓐ cling	Ⓑ bulge	Ⓒ operate	Ⓓ influence
Ⓔ fervent	Ⓕ exploit	Ⓖ decompose	

1. power   impact   effect   : _____
2. adhere   stick   bond   : _____
3. work   function   act   : _____
4. swelling   protrusion   bump   : _____
5. passionate   eager   enthusiastic : _____
6. abuse   take advantage misuse   : _____

C Choose the right meaning for each highlighted word.

1. The magnitude of loss caused by war is immeasurable.
   Ⓐ negative financial impact   Ⓑ level of seriousness and amount

2. Sam concluded that there was enough evidence and the decision was justly made.
   Ⓐ in an advantageous way   Ⓑ in a manner that is fair

3. Spring is the season when young animals are prone to the threat of hungry predators.
   Ⓐ vulnerable   Ⓑ having experience of something

4. The instructions for how to put this table together are quite straightforward.
   Ⓐ detailed and concrete   Ⓑ easy to understand or simple

5. Several history-changing ideas have emphasized the unfairness caused by the power of
   the aristocracy over the common people.
   Ⓐ a group of rich people   Ⓑ the upper class in society

Reference

Introduction

- Reference questions ask you to choose the word or phrase that a pronoun or other reference word in the passage refers to.

- Tested pronouns or reference words are highlighted within the passage.

- 0 to1 questions are given for each passage.

Question Types

- The word ☐ in the passage refers to

- The phrase ☐ in the passage refers to

Strategy

1. Check the form of the highlighted word: is it singular or plural, masculine or feminine, person or object?

2. Understand the context of the passage in relation to the object that the highlighted word or phrase refers to.

3. Check to see if the answer choice you have selected in place of the highlighted word or phrase flows naturally and is grammatically correct within the passage.

    • Pronouns or reference words that appear often
    ① Personal pronouns: they, their, them, it, its
    ② Demonstrative pronouns: this/that, these/those, the former/the latter
    ③ Indefinite pronouns: some, others, one, another, none, the other, any
    ④ Relative pronouns: who, whose, which, that
    ⑤ Demonstrative adverbs: there, then
    ⑥ Others: this/that + singular noun, these/those + plural noun, such + (a/an) + noun

● Basic Drills

The dime novel, called a *penny dreadful* in England, was a type of storybook that was popular in the late nineteenth century and sold for only a dime or a nickel a piece. The novels themselves were printed with paper covers, which made them cheaper and lighter than the leather-bound books common at that time. Dime novels became particularly popular in the early 1860s, during the U.S. Civil War, because they were very easy for soldiers to carry. The stories the books contained were sensational adventure tales with straightforward, formulaic plots. Critics condemned the stories as immoral due to their violent content, but the heroes in the novels often demonstrated positive character traits. They were brave, self-reliant, and patriotic. Dime novels were eventually replaced by pulp magazines, which featured similar stories, but the dime novel's influence can still be seen in modern publications like celebrity gossip tabloids and romance paperbacks.

1 The word them in the passage refers to

(A) dime novels   (B) leather-bound books   (C) soldiers   (D) paper covers

2 The word They in the passage refers to

(A) plots   (B) critics   (C) stories   (D) heroes in the novels

Made up of partially or wholly decayed organic matter, humus is the portion of soil that ranges from brown to black. Humus starts to form when organic residues of plants and animals decompose as they come in contact with microorganisms such as bacteria, fungi, and actinomycetes in soil. Carbon compounds in the residues are synthesized by the plant or animal when it is living, and these constitute energy for the various microbial life involved in the process of decay. During decomposition, humus's components are transformed so as to be usable by plants. Because it provides nutrients essential for plant growth, increases soil's water absorption, and improves soil workability, humus is prized by farmers and gardeners.

3 The word they in the passage refers to

(A) organic residues   (B) plants and animals   (C) microorganisms   (D) carbon compounds

4 The word it in the passage refers to

(A) decomposition   (B) humus   (C) plant   (D) soil

Vocabulary

Choose the word that is closest in meaning to the underlined word in the passage.

1. formulaic	(A) normal	(B) authorized	(C) authentic	(D) conventional
2. residues	(A) growths	(B) additions	(C) remains	(D) elements
3. constitute	(A) finish	(B) form	(C) enhance	(D) alter
4. prized	(A) awarded	(B) accumulated	(C) purchased	(D) valued

Reading Practice 01

When the supply of sediment at a river mouth exceeds the rate of its[1] removal by waves and tides, a buildup occurs. Normally taking the shape of a triangle in planar view, these deposits are known as deltas because they look like the Greek capital letter *delta* (Δ). In reality, many deltas do not exhibit the classic delta shape. A delta's shape can vary, mainly due to the energy associated with waves and currents. Deltas can be classified as wave-dominated, river-dominated, or tide- 5 dominated.

Wave-dominated deltas are little more than a bulge on the shoreline since there is so much wave activity that all sediment is spread evenly along the coast and does not accumulate at a river's end. Wave-dominated deltas have relatively smooth shorelines, which show a classic triangular shape with few <u>distributaries</u>. An example of such a delta is the Nile River Delta in 10 Egypt.

River-dominated deltas occur when there are large amounts of material in the river and both wave and tidal current energy on the coast are low. As the river meets the coast, its[2] discharge of water and sediment is little affected by waves and currents. Consequently, an irregular shaped delta with numerous distributaries is formed. One such example is the Mississippi Delta in the 15 United States.

Tide-dominated deltas typically occur in locations of large tidal ranges or high tidal current speeds. They have many branching channels and long narrow islands formed as tides and rivers flowed in different directions. Because in tide-dominated deltas sediment supply is overpowered by strong tidal currents, they tend to be very small. A famous example of such a process is the 20 Ganges-Brahmaputra Delta in Bangladesh.

Glossary

distributary: a river branch that flows away from the main stream

1 The word its[1] in the passage refers to

- (A) sediment
- (B) river mouth
- (C) buildup
- (D) shape

2 The word its[2] in the passage refers to

- (A) river-dominated delta
- (B) river
- (C) coast
- (D) sediment

3 The word they in the passage refers to

- (A) islands
- (B) tides and rivers
- (C) tide-dominated deltas
- (D) tidal currents

Extra Question

Which of the following is true about the characteristic of deltas?

- (A) Most deltas look like the Greek capital letter *delta*.
- (B) Wave-dominated deltas have smooth shorelines with few distributaries.
- (C) In river-dominated deltas, wave and tidal current energy is high.
- (D) Tide-dominated deltas have many islands with few branching channels.

Organization

- _____ — buildups of sediment at the mouth of a river
- Wave-dominated deltas ┬ classic _____ shape with few distributaries
  ├ sediment is spread _____
  └ an example is the Nile River Delta
- River-dominated deltas ┬ _____ shape with numerous distributaries
  ├ formed by large amounts of sediment in the river
  └ an example is the _____ Delta
- Tide-dominated deltas ┬ feature many _____ _____ and long narrow _____
  ├ small due to overpowered sediment supply
  └ an example is the Ganges-Brahmaputra Delta

Reading Practice 02

From the eighteenth century until the twentieth century, portraiture art reflected the changes occurring in colonial America. Initially, portraits were a staple of the aristocracy and were associated with luxury and monarchism. The portraits depicted wealthy and prominent individuals, and were a privilege only available to the elite. However, this changed dramatically after the American Revolution when it became apparent that portraiture could serve a more 5 practical function in terms of record keeping and for patriotic purposes. Portrait artists then went about painting America's leaders and founders, conveying notions of republicanism and modesty in their portrayals. This represented a break from traditional European portraiture which placed importance on portraying the elite status of its subjects. As the New Republic expanded and democracy flourished, portraiture became accessible, especially to the burgeoning middle class. 10 In the spirit of democracy, they sought to use this medium as a way of defining and reinforcing their identity, ideals, and place within the newly established society.

Soon, the rising demand for cheap portraits was met by the introduction of the silhouette portrait and the miniature portrait. Silhouette portraits were made by placing a person side-on to a piece of drawing paper tacked to the wall. A bright light such as a candle was used to create a 15 shadow of the person's profile on the white paper. This was then traced and cut. The process was complete when the silhouette was mounted and framed. Usually, these portraits were plain, but on occasion, paint was used as a means of decoration. Silhouettes, which became very fashionable between 1750 and 1850, were justly popular. Because they were cut from paper, they were an economically viable alternative to oil portraits. They were also very convenient – only one brief 20 sitting was required, and the whole process could be completed in just a few minutes.

Miniature portraits, which were popular between 1760 and 1840, were made by painting watercolor on small, thin ivory disks and could be worn as jewelry or framed. Because they were made by experts, they were more expensive than silhouettes but did bear a striking resemblance to their subject. These delicate pieces evolved to tiny oil portraits and began to increasingly take 25 on the qualities of photography, invented in 1839. However, as photographic methods gained a wider following and became more accessible to the general population, miniature portraits and silhouette portraits fell out of favor and became something of a lost art.

1   The word its in the passage refers to

(A) traditional European portraiture

(B) elite status

(C) New Republic

(D) democracy

2   The word they in the passage refers to

(A) portrait artists

(B) America's leaders and founders

(C) subjects

(D) the middle class

3   The phrase These delicate pieces in the passage refers to

(A) miniature portraits

(B) ivory disks

(C) silhouettes

(D) photographic methods

Extra Question

Which of the following is NOT true about silhouette portraits?

(A) They were always black and white.

(B) They were popular from 1750 to 1850.

(C) They usually included the shadow of one's profile.

(D) The manufacturing process was simple and cheap.

Summary

Portrait art during colonial America reflects its history. The _____ _____ changed the course of portraiture painting from a luxury item to a means of _____ _____ and a way of encouraging patriotism. The _____ _____ then used portraiture painting as a way of establishing their own identity within the newly formed democracy. _____ _____ and miniature portraits became fashionable because they were accessible. Silhouettes were convenient and affordable, while miniature portraits bore a close _____ to their subject. Due to the rise in photography, however, the popularity of these forms of portraiture declined.

● iBT Practice 01

The Erie Canal

In the aftermath of the American Revolution, it became clear that there was a need for a water route to connect the Great Lakes with the Atlantic coast to shorten travel time across New York State and promote commercial interests. To fill this void, the Erie Canal – a waterway 4 feet deep, 40 feet wide, and 363 miles long – connecting the Hudson River at Albany to Lake Erie at Buffalo was constructed. The most ambitious engineering project undertaken anywhere in the country up to that time, the canal was hailed as the greatest engineering wonder in the world and is still one of the largest canals in the United States.

➡ In order to open the western country to settlers and offer a cheap way to transport goods, the idea of a canal was put forward. However, the magnitude of undertaking such a project and the doubt of the state's ability to cope with the difficulties led to fervent opposition. DeWitt Clinton, then mayor of New York City, supported the construction of the canal, and when he became governor of New York State in 1817, funds for a canal from the Hudson River to the Great Lakes were hastily approved. After eight years of construction, the canal opened on October 26, 1825, with a formal ceremony generally known as the "Marriage of the Waters" between the Great Lakes and the Atlantic. The first fleet to travel its entire length was headed by the boat *Seneca Chief*, bearing Governor Clinton and a company of distinguished citizens.

➡ The canal was an immediate commercial and financial success: the cost of transporting products from Buffalo to New York City decreased by more than 90%, shortening travel time by half. Buffalo became a major trans-shipment point as farm produce from western states and Canada flowed through the city on its way to New York City. New York City became the commercial, financial, and immigration heart of the country, with five times as many people following commercial interests in New York as there were before the completion of the Erie Canal. Within nine years, the tolls collected from the canal covered the entire construction cost and funded several branch canals in the state.

For many years the canal was a profitable route, but beginning in the 1850s, its advantages in the area of long-distance transport were eventually destroyed due to increasing competition from railroads and highways. Following the opening of the St. Lawrence Seaway in 1959, the canal system experienced a serious decline in commercial traffic in the latter part of the twentieth century.

1. The word void in the passage is closest in meaning to

    Ⓐ gap   Ⓑ project   Ⓒ desire   Ⓓ trade

2. The phrase put forward in the passage is closest in meaning to

    Ⓐ started   Ⓑ proposed   Ⓒ settled   Ⓓ needed

3. According to paragraph 2, the idea of the Erie Canal was met with strong opposition because of

    Ⓐ the amount of money that would be needed to operate the canal

    Ⓑ a lack of skilled workers to complete the canal

    Ⓒ the state's perceived inability to deal with such a large project

    Ⓓ the damage the canal would do to traditional businesses

    Paragraph 2 is marked with an arrow [➡].

4. Which of the sentences below best expresses the essential information in the highlighted sentence in the passage? *Incorrect* choices change the meaning in important ways or leave out essential information.

    Ⓐ The Erie Canal resulted in New York becoming the most important business and immigration center in the country and a boom in population.

    Ⓑ The construction of the canal led to more immigrants becoming involved in the financial industries.

    Ⓒ The opening of the Erie Canal resulted in a huge increase in the population of New York City.

    Ⓓ The Erie Canal made New York City the commercial capital of the nation by increasing domestic trade.

5. According to paragraph 3, which of the following is an effect of the Erie Canal?

    Ⓐ Increased farm produce

    Ⓑ Revived local businesses

    Ⓒ Reduced travel time

    Ⓓ Increased tourism

    Paragraph 3 is marked with an arrow [➡].

6. The word **its** in the passage refers to

    (A) New York State　　　　　　　　(B) Erie Canal

    (C) area of long-distance transport　(D) St. Lawrence Seaway

7. **Directions:** An introductory sentence for a brief summary of the passage is provided below. Complete the summary by selecting the THREE answer choices that express the most important ideas in the passage. Some sentences do not belong in the summary because they express ideas that are not presented in the passage or are minor ideas in the passage. ***This question is worth 2 points.***

    ┌──┐
    │ The Erie Canal was constructed in 1825 as an important water route in New York State. │
    │   │
    │ •   │
    │   │
    │ •   │
    │   │
    │ •   │
    └──┘

    Answer Choices

    (A) The canal was hailed as one of the engineering wonders of the world upon its opening.

    (B) It was designed as a way to shorten travel time and promote commercial interests.

    (C) Tolls collected from the canal recovered some of the construction costs.

    (D) Governor DeWitt Clinton and other distinguished citizens were the first passengers to travel the canal's entire length.

    (E) Competition from railroads, highways, and the St. Lawrence Seaway led to the downfall of the canal.

    (F) The canal was an immediate success and led to a surge in business.

    Drag your answer choices to the spaces where they belong. To remove an answer choice, click on it. To review the passage, click on **View Text**.

iBT Practice 02

The Great Hunger

➡ The Great Hunger, often referred to as the Irish Potato Famine, began in 1845 when about half of the potato crop in Ireland was infected with a fungus-like organism and made inedible. The Great Hunger lasted for seven years and devastated the poor Irish tenant farmers who depended on the potato crop as their main source of food and income. Because these farmers depended on this crop for almost all of their food, the rural poor in Ireland were quickly faced with a damaging ₅ crisis.

➡ The ruined potato crop was a disaster, but the suffering of the Irish people was made much worse by the social and political conditions in Ireland in the mid-nineteenth century. ■ They sold a portion of the crops that they grew to pay rent to their landlords and survived by eating whatever food was left from their harvests. ■ When the potato crops failed, these farmers had no ₁₀ food to eat and no money to pay rent with. ■ Many farmers were evicted from their homes, and most poor families struggled with starvation. ■

These farmers looked to their government for assistance, but they received little help. At that time, Ireland was controlled by the British government, and the British were not willing to give active financial aid to the Irish. The British government initially set up soup kitchens to provide free ₁₅ meals to the poor. They were an effective and relatively cheap solution to the famine. However, the government in London worried that the Irish poor would become dependent on British assistance, so they closed the soup kitchens in 1847.

➡ Another measure Britain took was to remove tariffs on imported food and grain. The government's goal was to make bread more affordable in Ireland. The repeal of these tariffs did ₂₀ make more food available for purchase, particularly cornmeal from North America. This coarse flour was even sold to the poor at a discount. But it was not an effective long-term solution because poor Irish farmers simply had no money to buy food with.

What made matters worse was that large amounts of food produced in Ireland continued to be exported. Records show that exports of items like livestock and butter even increased during ₂₅ the famine. Many poor people were left to starve.

The Great Hunger ended in 1852 when the potato crop recovered in Ireland. But the damage done to the Irish society could not be reversed. Roughly one million people died during the Great Hunger, either of starvation or of diseases caused by malnutrition. It is estimated that another 2.5 million Irish people fled their homes and immigrated to new lands to escape poverty. ₃₀

1. The word tenant in the passage is closest in meaning to

    Ⓐ renter   Ⓑ employer

    Ⓒ settler   Ⓓ prisoner

2. In paragraph 1, the author mentions that Irish farmers depended on the potato crop for almost all
    of their food in order to

    Ⓐ highlight the mismanagement of the food supply

    Ⓑ explain the dangers of relying on a single crop for survival

    Ⓒ emphasize how serious the loss of the potato crop was

    Ⓓ give an example of the typical lifestyle of an Irish farmer

    Paragraph 1 is marked with an arrow [➡].

3. According to paragraph 2, the failure of the potato crop resulted in all of the following EXCEPT

    Ⓐ rural people not having enough food to eat

    Ⓑ a migration from the countryside to the cities

    Ⓒ tenant farmers being unable to earn money

    Ⓓ poor families being kicked out of their homes

    Paragraph 2 is marked with an arrow [➡].

4. The word They in the passage refers to

    Ⓐ British government

    Ⓑ Irish farmers

    Ⓒ financial aids

    Ⓓ soup kitchens

5. According to paragraph 4, why was discounted cornmeal not an effective long-term solution to
    the Great Hunger?

    Ⓐ The tariffs imposed by the British made cornmeal unaffordable.

    Ⓑ It was too expensive to ship goods from North America to Ireland.

    Ⓒ The people suffering from the famine did not have any money.

    Ⓓ Cornmeal was not nutritious enough to replace potatoes in a diet.

    Paragraph 4 is marked with an arrow [➡].

6. Look at the four squares [■] that indicate where the following sentence could be added to the passage.

    Most poor farmers lived on land that they did not own.

    Where would the sentence best fit?

    Click on a square [■] to add the sentence to the passage.

7. **Directions:** An introductory sentence for a brief summary of the passage is provided below. Complete the summary by selecting the THREE answer choices that express the most important ideas in the passage. Some sentences do not belong in the summary because they express ideas that are not presented in the passage or are minor ideas in the passage. *This question is worth 2 points.*

    The Great Hunger was a disastrous famine that was worsened by the social and political systems of nineteenth-century Ireland.

    -
    -
    -

Answer Choices

(A) Poor Irish farmers lived on rented land and relied on the potato crop as their main source of food and often their only way to earn money.

(B) When the potato crop was ruined, not only did the Irish farmers have nothing to eat, they also could not pay rent, leaving many families starving and homeless.

(C) The British government spent heavily to provide for the safety and well-being of the Irish citizens it was responsible for.

(D) The famine lasted seven years, and due to the government's inadequate response, nearly a million Irish died and millions more fled the island.

(E) The free soup kitchens created a class of people in Irish society that depended on the government to supply their basic needs.

(F) Many Irish people immigrated to North America in order to escape poverty.

    Drag your answer choices to the spaces where they belong. To remove an
    answer choice, click on it. To review the passage, click on **View Text**.

Actual **Practice Test**

Symbiotic Relationships

Symbiosis is derived from the Greek word simply meaning "living together" and is used to describe an association between two organisms. When at least two individuals representing two different species live and interact closely in a manner that benefits either or both species, symbiosis is occurring. Symbiotic interrelationships can be broken into three main categories: mutualism, where both species involved benefit from the relationship; parasitism, when one species gains and the other is damaged in the process; and commensalism, in which one species benefits and the other is not affected. 5

➡ Mutualism can be witnessed across many different species, but a famous instance of symbiosis occurs between the Egyptian plover and the crocodile. ■ The plover is known for feeding on parasites that live on crocodiles, and hence, the crocodile is happy for the bird to hunt on its body. ■ For the bird, this relationship not only provides food but also safety as predators are unlikely to strike at the bird so close to its host. ■ Most forms of mutualism are facultative, meaning the partners can survive apart successfully, but some cases of mutualism are so close that the interacting species are unable to live without each other – these are known as obligate relationships. ■ 10 15

Parasites are organisms that cannot survive without their host. The host species is always exploited to some degree in a parasitic relationship, but often in a way where its health is only slowly damaged, which means the parasite can exploit its host over a longer period. Parasitism is divided into two branches: ectoparasitism and endoparasitism. Whereas ectoparasites live outside of their host, endoparasites refer to those animals that live inside the body of the host. The fish doctor is an example of an ectoparasite. The fish doctor clings to a fish's fins, scales, or gills. Then, it sucks its host's blood until that fish dies. The connection between the pearlfish and sea cucumbers is one example of an endoparasitic relationship. As a sea cucumber takes part in gas exchange and breathes in water, the pearlfish enters its body. It shelters in daytime, exiting at night to feed on small fish. Young pearlfish even consume the respiratory structures of the sea cucumber. The sea cucumber suffers a lot of stress because of its relationship with the pearlfish so attempts to expel it by getting rid of its own digestive tract. This process can hurt the sea cucumber a lot. 20 25

➡ Commensalism is a relationship between two living organisms where one party benefits and the other is neither harmed nor helped. These relationships vary in strength and duration from very close, long-lived symbiosis to short, weak interactions. Commensalism usually happens between a species that is prone to being attacked, or with poor locomotive skills, and another species with an effective system of defense. One example is the clownfish, which finds safety by swimming close to sea anemones, whose tentacles contain stinging cells to keep predators away. 30

This helps protect the clownfish, and the anemone is not bothered by its guest's presence.   35

➡ There may be a number of species competing within one microenvironment, but through symbiosis each can exist in harmony with the other and a sustainable balance can be reached. Whether it is a mutualistic, parasitic, or commensalistic relationship, symbiosis is an illustration of nature's ability to operate efficiently.

1. The word association in the passage is closest in meaning to
   Ⓐ division   Ⓑ evolution
   Ⓒ connection   Ⓓ trait

2. What can be inferred from paragraph 2 about obligate mutualism?
   Ⓐ Through obligate mutualism, evolution in different species is possible.
   Ⓑ The stronger partner enjoys more benefits than the weaker partner.
   Ⓒ The lives of both participants would be worse if the relationship were broken.
   Ⓓ Obligate mutualism is the strongest relationship across different species.
   Paragraph 2 is marked with an arrow [➡].

3. Which of the sentences below best expresses the essential information in the highlighted sentence in the passage? *Incorrect* choices change the meaning in important ways or leave out essential information.
   Ⓐ A parasite always exploits its host over a long period of time.
   Ⓑ A parasite often exploits its host in order to damage its health.
   Ⓒ A parasite stops exploiting its host after a certain period of time.
   Ⓓ A parasite always exploits its host but often gradually over time.

4. Why does the author mention the fish doctor?
   Ⓐ To show how one party exploits the host while living outside of its host
   Ⓑ To demonstrate similarities between ectoparasitism and endoparasitism
   Ⓒ To illustrate how fast the parasite can harm its host
   Ⓓ To identify the method one party uses to kill another

5. The word It in the passage refers to

   (A) endoparasitic relationship   (B) sea cucumber

   (C) gas exchange   (D) pearlfish

6. The word expel in the passage is closest in meaning to

   (A) pick out   (B) take in

   (C) drive out   (D) cut off

7. According to paragraph 4, all of the following are mentioned about the relationship between clownfish and sea anemones EXCEPT

   (A) The clownfish swims close to sea anemones to get protection from other predators.

   (B) The sea anemone helps the clownfish with its stinging cells to form a defense system.

   (C) The clownfish uses the sea anemone as a locomotive device.

   (D) The sea anemone is not affected by the behavior of the clownfish.

   Paragraph 4 is marked with an arrow [➡].

8. According to paragraph 5, what is the effect of symbiosis?

   (A) It provides a way for living organisms to exist in a natural balance.

   (B) It helps species to compete with each other in small-sized environments.

   (C) Nature's self-purification system can be operated efficiently.

   (D) It helps to keep the number of species competing within an environment low.

   Paragraph 5 is marked with an arrow [➡].

9. Look at the four squares [■] that indicate where the following sentence could be added to the passage.

   It even opens its jaws to let the bird enter its mouth safely to hunt.

   Where would the sentence best fit?

   Click on a square [■] to add the sentence to the passage.

10. **Directions:** Complete the table by matching the statements below. Select the appropriate statements from the answer choices and match them to the type of symbiotic relationships to which they relate. TWO of the answer choices will NOT be used. *This question is worth 3 points.*

Drag your answer choices to the spaces where they belong. To remove an answer choice, click on it. To review the passage, click on **View Text**.

Answer Choices	Mutualism
(A) One example is the relationship between sea anemones and clownfish. ▶ ▶	
(B) Both parties derive benefits from the relationship.	
(C) There are two categories according to whether one party lives inside or outside of the host's body.	Parasitism
(D) Both parties collaborate to attract their prey. ▶	
(E) Pearlfish exploit their hosts while they are in the hosts' body. ▶	
(F) There are facultative and obligate forms according to the degree of dependence.	Commensalism
(G) The Egyptian plover benefits from symbiosis, whereas the crocodile remains unaffected. ▶	

Organization

Symbiotic Relationships

Symbiosis

- _____ between two species that is beneficial to one or both of the creatures
- Three categories: mutualism, parasitism, and commensalism

Mutualism

- Both species benefit.
- _____ _____ feed on parasites that live on crocodiles.
- Two types of mutualism: facultative and _____ relationships

Parasitism

- Parasites rely on their hosts, which are _____ by the relationship.
- Ectoparasite: a fish doctor clings to a fish's fins, scales, or gills and sucks its blood until the fish dies
- _____: a pearlfish lives inside the sea cucumber

Commensalism

- One creature _____ from the relationship, while the other remains unaffected.
- _____ swim close to sea anemones.

Conclusion

- _____ serves as an example of nature's ability to operate efficiently.

Vocabulary Review

A **Fill in the blanks with the best answer. Change the form if necessary.**

discharge	locomotive	hail	profile	immoral	gossip

1. The snail's foot muscle is its main _____ organ.
2. Standing in a line, he turned around and saw the _____ of the man behind him.
3. Animal abuse is not considered an _____ act to those who care only about human beings.
4. It is unwise to believe all the _____ constantly fed by the media.
5. In 2002, critics _____ the book as being an "original and insightful translation of life in American suburbs."

B **Choose the word or phrase that is closest in meaning to each highlighted word.**

1. The vase has a colorful and delicate flower pattern.
   Ⓐ various   Ⓑ splendid   Ⓒ fine   Ⓓ small

2. The reason for the toll increase on the road was a mystery and an annoyance to Jeff.
   Ⓐ fee   Ⓑ noise   Ⓒ traffic   Ⓓ danger

3. As snow accumulated on the road, the traffic was severely disrupted.
   Ⓐ melted   Ⓑ built up   Ⓒ froze   Ⓓ let down

4. The coming of spring means respiratory problems for those suffering from allergies.
   Ⓐ medical   Ⓑ breathing   Ⓒ environmental   Ⓓ financial

5. The planar diagram of the classroom was so well-proportioned that it almost looked 3D.
   Ⓐ realistic   Ⓑ outstanding   Ⓒ precise   Ⓓ two-dimensional

6. In a country ruled by a dictator, whether or not a citizen is patriotic is usually of great concern.
   Ⓐ loyal   Ⓑ educated   Ⓒ resistant   Ⓓ opinionated

7. Artists use symbols to convey their message to the masses effectively.
   Ⓐ sell   Ⓑ display   Ⓒ define   Ⓓ transmit

C **Choose the correct word in each sentence.**

1. The (debt, delta) is extremely interesting for the variety of plant and animal life that it supports.
2. Her suggestion is completely (viable, visible) if you look at it from a different point of view.
3. Mr. Scott thinks (modification, modesty) is a desirable characteristic in a person.

UNIT

03

Fact & Negative Fact

Vocabulary Preview

A **Choose the word that best matches each definition.**

> (A) counterpart (B) stimulus (C) instability
>
> (D) column (E) corpse (F) consensus

1. a dead person's body: _____
2. general opinion or decision made by a group: _____
3. something with a vertical, narrow shape: _____
4. something that causes a response: _____
5. something or someone with a similar purpose or characteristics: _____

B **Choose the best synonym for each list of words.**

> (A) vertical (B) venue (C) assume (D) distinct
>
> (E) orderly (F) property (G) display

1. characteristic	feature	attribute	: _____
2. presume	suppose	believe	: _____
3. site	location	setting	: _____
4. organized	regular	systematic	: _____
5. perpendicular	straight	upright	: _____
6. unique	different	exceptional	: _____

C **Choose the right meaning for each highlighted word or phrase.**

1. The artists contend that they need more grants to fund their projects.
   - (A) to state strongly
   - (B) to campaign for something

2. After investigating, we found that the two specimens did not share the same chromosomal arrangements.
   - (A) display in a particular order
   - (B) regular position

3. The waste pile was leveled off and compacted by the machine.
   - (A) to drop down just a little
   - (B) to make even or smooth

4. Even though the explorers had not been looking for the hidden ancient cave, they stumbled upon it.
   - (A) to discover by chance
   - (B) to start the observation of

5. The stunning beauty of the canyon and surrounding mountains more than satisfied the family's expectations.
   - (A) natural
   - (B) striking

Fact & Negative Fact

Introduction

Factual Information
- Factual Information questions require you to select the right answer to questions concerning important details mentioned in the passage.
- 1 to 3 questions are given for each passage.

Negative Fact
- Unlike Factual Information questions, Negative Fact questions require you to choose the answer choice that provides incorrect information about important details referred to in the passage or information not mentioned in the passage.
- 0 to 2 questions are given for each passage.

Question Types

Factual Information
- According to the passage, which of the following is true about X?
- According to paragraph ___, when / how / why …?
- In paragraph ___, the author states that

Negative Fact
- According to the passage, which of the following is NOT true about X?
- Which of the following is NOT mentioned as X?
- All of the following are mentioned as X EXCEPT

Strategy

1. Quickly scan the passage to locate the key word or phrase from each answer choice. Read the sentence that contains the key word or phrase and figure out the context, and compare it to each answer choice.

2. Eliminate incorrect answer choices and choose the correct one from the remaining answer choices.

   ### Factual Information
   • The correct answer paraphrases the information within the passage.

   ### Negative Fact
   • The correct answer has information not mentioned in the passage, information mentioned in the passage but irrelevant to the question, or information that incorrectly describes parts of the passage.

Basic Drills

The state of awareness which involves concentrating on a particular aspect of the environment while ignoring other aspects is known as selective attention. An experiment was carried out to demonstrate how selective attention operates. In the experiment, participants looked at a video of two ball-passing games. One team of players wore white uniforms; the other wore black. The participants in the experiment had to determine the number of passes occurring between members wearing black uniforms. During the games, a woman with an umbrella suddenly walked across the basketball court where the players were competing. The woman could clearly be seen for four seconds. When asked about the video, only 21% of the participants said they saw the woman with the umbrella. This is because of selective attention filtering out part of the stimulus. This process does not only occur in visual stimulus but generally happens across perception.

1   According to the passage, fewer participants were aware of the presence of the woman because

Ⓐ they were not concentrating properly on the games

Ⓑ her image was too vague to be identified among various stimuli

Ⓒ focusing on a specific aspect prevented them from perceiving other aspects

Ⓓ recognizing the visual stimulus was the most difficult aspect

Derived from an Old Norse word meaning "corpse man," the name *narwhal* was coined because the adult narwhal whale has a white and gray coloring and possesses the ability to lie belly-up for several minutes without moving much. Having a short head and hardly any snout, it has no dorsal fin, but has a long, low dorsal hump. The outstanding feature of male narwhals is their single amazingly long tusk that sticks out from the left side of the upper jaw and grows in a long spiral. This tusk can grow to three meters in length, compared with a body length of four to five meters, and weigh up to ten kilograms. The female narwhal may also produce a tusk, although this is quite uncommon. The reason why narwhals grow tusks is uncertain – scientists have speculated that it may help transmit sound, establish social dominance, and find food.

2   According to the passage, all of the following are mentioned about the narwhal tusk EXCEPT

Ⓐ it may be used for social dominance   Ⓑ it is shaped like a spiral horn

Ⓒ female narwhals may possess a tusk   Ⓓ it is white and gray in color

Vocabulary

Choose the word that is closest in meaning to the underlined word in the passage.

1. awareness	Ⓐ fear	Ⓑ fatigue	Ⓒ confusion	Ⓓ consciousness
2. filtering	Ⓐ removing	Ⓑ emphasizing	Ⓒ feeding	Ⓓ stopping
3. coined	Ⓐ fixed	Ⓑ created	Ⓒ changed	Ⓓ improved
4. dominance	Ⓐ friendliness	Ⓑ development	Ⓒ debate	Ⓓ power

Eratosthenes was a third-century BC Greek mathematician who served as the chief librarian in the library of Alexandria, Egypt, one of the great learning centers of the ancient world. Among his many achievements, he is perhaps best remembered for using his knowledge of mathematics and geometry to calculate the distance of the earth's circumference.

➡ Eratosthenes began with the knowledge that the sun cast no shadow at noon on June 5 21 – the summer solstice – in the city of Syene, while in Alexandria, due north of Syene, the sun always cast a shadow. This observation by itself showed that the earth was spherical, based on the assumption that the sun's rays run parallel when they reach the earth, and he realized it could be used to deduce the earth's circumference. He then measured the angles of the shadows of vertical sticks in Alexandria on the same day and time, which proved to be slanted at an angle 10 7 degrees from vertical. He decided this angle was congruent to the angle at the earth's center between Syene and Alexandria. Since this was about one-fiftieth of a full circle, which is 360 degrees, the distance between Syene and Alexandria must be one-fiftieth of the circumference of the earth. He estimated the distance between the two cities to be 5,000 *stadia*, an ancient Greek unit of measurement, and assuming that the earth was 50 times larger, concluded that its 15 circumference was approximately 250,000 stadia.

➡ Eratosthenes's calculations were not without flaws, including an error in his estimate of the distance between Alexandria and Syene. Also, there is no consensus on the exact length of the Greek measurement stadia, which Eratosthenes used to make his calculations. Despite all this, his final conclusion was astonishingly accurate. Using modern units of measurement, 20 Eratosthenes's calculations convert to approximately 25,000–28,900 miles, a stunning conclusion considering that we now know the circumference of the Earth to be 24,903 miles.

1   According to paragraph 2, the shadow observed in Alexandria while there was no shadow occurring in Syene proved that

Ⓐ the earth is round

Ⓑ Syene is located south of Alexandria

Ⓒ solar rays run parallel upon reaching the earth

Ⓓ June 21 is the longest day of the year

Paragraph 2 is marked with an arrow [➡].

2   According to paragraph 3, why is there no exact translation of Eratosthenes's calculation to "miles"?

Ⓐ Because he did not make a record of the various calculations that he made

Ⓑ Because he used secret codes to record his calculation

Ⓒ Because he made errors when he measured the distance

Ⓓ Because the exact length of the stadia that he used is unclear

Paragraph 3 is marked with an arrow [➡].

3   Which of the following is NOT true about the process that Eratosthenes used to measure the circumference of the earth?

Ⓐ He measured the angles of the shadows cast by vertical sticks in Alexandria.

Ⓑ He measured the approximate distance between Syene and Alexandria.

Ⓒ He calculated the angle at the earth's center between Syene and Alexandria.

Ⓓ He multiplied the distance between Syene and Alexandria by the central angle between them.

Summary

The third-century BC Greek mathematician Eratosthenes is best known for accurately calculating the earth's _____. By comparing shadows cast by the sun on the _____ _____, Eratosthenes deduced that the earth is round in shape. He furthered this observation, calculating the earth's circumference by measuring the _____ of the shadows cast by vertical sticks in the city of _____. By comparing this angle with the 360 degrees of a globe, he concluded that the earth's circumference was _____ _____ larger than the distance between Syene and Alexandria. Although the calculations had some flaws, his results were incredibly accurate, as demonstrated by modern calculations.

Reading Practice 02

A thunderstorm is a heavy rain shower that includes thunder and lightning and is usually accompanied by strong surface winds. An average thunderstorm measures 15 miles in diameter and keeps going for approximately 30 minutes. A thunderstorm develops when there are three basic ingredients – moisture, rising unstable air, and a force to lift this rising air – that cause instability in the atmosphere. The life cycle of a thunderstorm can be divided into three stages: the cumulus stage, the mature stage, and the dissipating stage. 5

➡ The first stage of a thunderstorm is the cumulus stage. During daylight hours, the sun heating the earth's surface causes the air to warm. This lighter warm air begins to rise – known as an *updraft* – and then cools, eventually condensing into a cumulus cloud. As the cumulus cloud keeps growing vertically as warm air keeps rising, it resembles a tower. During this short, devel- opmental stage, there is little or no rain because water droplets and ice crystals are kept hanging in the cloud by the updraft. As the cloud reaches heights of below-freezing temperatures, cloud particles begin to increase in size. Eventually, the water droplets start to fall as they become too heavy for the updraft to hold up. 10

➡ As soon as precipitation begins to fall, the thunderstorm has entered its mature stage. At this time, a warm updraft continues to feed the storm, but a column of the cold air known as a *downdraft* also begins to push downward. During the mature stage, the cloud grows to as high as 20,000 meters, reaching a stable atmospheric zone, and cannot rise any further. The top of the cloud is leveled off, forming an <u>anvil</u> shape. A thunderstorm is at its strongest near the end of the mature stage, with rain at its heaviest and gusty winds, hail, frequent lightning, and even tornadoes occurring. 15 20

➡ Within 30 minutes of entering the mature stage, the thunderstorm starts to dissipate. As a large amount of rainfall is produced, the downdraft strengthens and cuts off the updraft and inflow of moist air. As moist air can no longer rise, precipitation can no longer form, so rainfall eventually ends. 25

Glossary

anvil: an iron block on which heated metals are beaten and shaped by a hammer

1   According to paragraph 2, there is no precipitation produced in the cumulus stage because

        Ⓐ there is a lack of moisture contained within the cloud

        Ⓑ the tower-like shape of the cloud prevents water droplets and ice crystals from escaping

        Ⓒ cloud particles are too small in size to allow rain to fall

        Ⓓ the updraft results in water droplets and ice crystals being retained in the cloud

        Paragraph 2 is marked with an arrow [➡].

2   All of the following are mentioned in paragraph 3 about the mature stage EXCEPT

        Ⓐ a column of cold air presses down on the storm

        Ⓑ the cloud reaches its maximum height during this stage

        Ⓒ the updraft stops influencing the storm

        Ⓓ the storm is at its strongest at the end of this stage

        Paragraph 3 is marked with an arrow [➡].

3   According to paragraph 4, which of the following is true about the dissipating stage?

        Ⓐ Moist air no longer flows into the cloud.

        Ⓑ It begins at least 30 minutes after the mature stage.

        Ⓒ Rainfall is maintained at a steady rate.

        Ⓓ The speed of the downdraft slightly decreases.

        Paragraph 4 is marked with an arrow [➡].

Organization

- A thunderstorm — a heavy _____ _____ with thunder, lightning, and strong surface winds
- Three stages of the thunderstorm formation
  - The cumulus stage ── begins when a warm updraft forms a(n) _____ _____
    - little or no rain
  - The mature stage ── begins when _____ starts to fall
    - an updraft of warm air and a downdraft of _____ air are present
    - the peak of the storm, with heavy rain and frequent _____
  - The dissipating stage ── begins within _____ _____ of the mature stage
    - the storm ends as the updraft and moist air are cut off by the downdraft

iBT Practice 01

The Distinct Fremont Culture

→ The Fremont people were a pre-Columbian archaeological culture which existed between 400 and 1300 AD. They were named after the Fremont River in Utah where the first Fremont sites were discovered. The culture was characterized by small-scale, scattered communities whose primary means of subsistence was farming. They were originally considered to be a part of the neighboring Anasazi culture, but are now considered to be a distinct culture that migrated into the 5 area which encompasses present-day Utah.

In fact, there are several artifact categories of the Fremont culture which mark it as distinct. For instance, they developed a particular way of making baskets called one-rod-and-bundle baskets in which fibers were wrapped around one rod which circled the basket. Some archaeologists contend that Fremont culture can be defined on the basis of this artifact alone 10 because it differed markedly from the way in which the Anasazi constructed baskets.

Moccasin and clay figurines are other artifacts that distinguish the Fremont culture from others that existed at the same time. Moccasins were constructed from the hock of deer or sheep leg which formed the heel of the shoe. This style of moccasin differs greatly from the woven sandals of the Anasazi. Similarly, the clay figurines, which were three-dimensional and used for 15 ceremonial rites, were also unique. Human shaped and adorned with necklaces made from bone and stone, they display a high level of artistry.

Another important piece of evidence that shows Fremont culture was unique is their thin-walled gray pottery. The pottery, which has stayed intact over hundreds of years, is what ties the scattered Fremont tribes together. What distinguishes this pottery is the material from which it is 20 made. The Fremont added various kinds of granular rock and sand to wet clay to insure even drying and to prevent cracking.

→ The Fremont culture vanished sometime between 1250 and 1500 AD. Although the exact reasons for their disappearance are unknown, many scholars concur that it was caused by the migration of other tribes. Because they were full-time hunter-gatherers, it is likely that these tribes 25 displaced the part-time Fremont hunter-gatherers by competing for scarce resources. The fact that classic Fremont artifacts were replaced with different styles of basketry, pottery, and art at this time indicates that the Fremont people were indeed driven out of the region and replaced by a migrating tribe.

Glossary

Anasazi culture: a Native American culture which flourished in the U.S. Southwest and whose descendants are the modern Pueblo peoples

VOLUME 🔊   HELP ?   OK ✔   NEXT ▶

1. The word encompasses in the passage is closest in meaning to
    Ⓐ influences   Ⓑ includes   Ⓒ borders   Ⓓ overlooks

2. All of the following are mentioned in paragraph 1 about the Fremont culture EXCEPT
    Ⓐ its sites were discovered in Utah
    Ⓑ it existed from 400 to 1300 AD
    Ⓒ it was characterized by small-scale communities
    Ⓓ it originated from the Anasazi culture
    Paragraph 1 is marked with an arrow [➡].

3. Why does the author mention the woven sandals of the Anasazi?
    Ⓐ To give an example of the artistic skills of Anasazi culture
    Ⓑ To show how they were influenced by the Fremont culture
    Ⓒ To illustrate special weaving skills not possessed by the Fremont culture
    Ⓓ To provide a point of contrast that shows the unique nature of the Fremont culture

4. The word they in the passage refers to
    Ⓐ clay figurines   Ⓑ ceremonial rites   Ⓒ necklaces   Ⓓ Fremont people

5. The word concur in the passage is closest in meaning to
    Ⓐ debate   Ⓑ consider   Ⓒ agree   Ⓓ criticize

6. According to paragraph 5, what evidence is there that the Fremont people were driven out of the region?
    Ⓐ The disappearance of tools they used for hunting
    Ⓑ The development of a new pottery style found in the region
    Ⓒ The construction of Fremont-style housing in neighboring areas
    Ⓓ The presence of different styles of artifacts that seemed to replace Fremont artifacts
    Paragraph 5 is marked with an arrow [➡].

7. **Directions:** An introductory sentence for a brief summary of the passage is provided below. Complete the summary by selecting the THREE answer choices that express the most important ideas in the passage. Some sentences do not belong in the summary because they express ideas that are not presented in the passage or are minor ideas in the passage. ***This question is worth 2 points.***

> The Fremont developed a number of unique artifacts which mark the Fremont culture as distinct.
>
> •
>
> •
>
> •

Answer Choices

(A) Fremont pottery decorated with black paint is a unique artifact of Fremont culture.

(B) The Fremont wore moccasins constructed from animal legs and made human-shaped clay figurines for ceremonial purposes.

(C) The Fremont people are considered to be the most advanced Native tribe that lived in the Utah area.

(D) Though the early techniques of making moccasins and clay figurines were influenced by Anasazi culture, the Fremont developed them further.

(E) The Fremont's unique style of basket weaving can be used to identify their culture.

(F) When the Fremont made pottery, they used materials distinct from those used in Anasazi pottery.

> Drag your answer choices to the spaces where they belong. To remove an answer choice, click on it. To review the passage, click on **View Text**.

iBT Practice 02

History of the Periodic Table

➡ The periodic table of elements is an arrangement of chemical elements and their symbols into columns and rows. It shows the relationship between the elements, and each element's atomic number increases as you move from the top left to the bottom right side of the table. Even before its creation, researchers during the Enlightenment period had already built up vast amounts of elemental knowledge. By 1689, a total of 63 elements had been identified, and as 5 they were, patterns between them began to emerge.

To better predict chemical behavior, scientists began organizing these elements in a table based on their properties. One of the earliest among them was the German chemist Johannes Dobereiner, who in the early nineteenth century, proposed the idea of grouping elements in sets of three that share similar properties. One example of such a triad was gold, silver, and copper. 10 But his theory could not be applied to many other elements of the time, and so it was eventually discarded.

The next evolution of the table came in the mid-nineteenth century when English chemist John Newlands suggested his law of octaves. The atomic masses of many elements became known by this time, which probably led Newlands to hypothesize that chemical behavior was 15 directly related to an element's mass. He therefore arranged the elements in order of increasing atomic mass and realized that elemental properties were similar on every seventh element, similar to octaves in music. The idea was later rejected, however, since it only worked with elements lighter than calcium.

➡ The modern periodic table as we know it today was first published by Dmitri Mendeleev 20 in 1869. Unlike others, Mendeleev correctly predicted that some elements were still undiscovered. For this reason he didn't fill out blanks in his table corresponding to atomic masses 44, 68, 72, and 100, spots which would later be filled by scandium, gallium, germanium, and technetium. He also repositioned certain elements in previous tables after observing the atomic masses assigned to beryllium, indium, and uranium were inaccurate. 25

Missing from Mendeleev's table, however, were the noble gases, which Sir William Ramsay discovered between 1894 and 1898, the first of which was argon, which had an atomic mass of 40. Because this mass was similar to potassium's but greater than chlorine's, he decided to insert the noble gases between the alkali metals and halogens. But it would be British physicist H. G. J. Mosely, who by studying the frequencies of X-rays emitted by the elements in 1913, demonstrated 30 that the elements were better arranged according to their atomic number rather than their atomic mass, thereby providing a theoretical framework beyond Mendeleev's simple observations.

1. What can be inferred from paragraph 1 about scientists from the Enlightenment period?
   Ⓐ They recognized the significance of the atomic number.
   Ⓑ They concluded there were only 63 elements in total.
   Ⓒ They were unaware of any connections between the elements.
   Ⓓ They conducted research without the use of the periodic table.
   Paragraph 1 is marked with an arrow [➡].

2. The author mentions gold, silver, and copper in order to
   Ⓐ explain why a theory failed to be accepted
   Ⓑ show elements which have properties that are alike
   Ⓒ contrast them with other elements of that time
   Ⓓ identify three newly discovered elements

3. Which of the sentences below best expresses the essential information in the highlighted sentence in the passage? *Incorrect* choices change the meaning in important ways or leave out essential information.
   Ⓐ The masses of many elements were unknown in the mid-nineteenth century, so Newlands tried to calculate their masses.
   Ⓑ Newlands's interpretation of the elements was likely influenced by the fact that many atomic masses had already been revealed.
   Ⓒ According to Newlands, the product of a chemical reaction is based on the masses of the elements involved.
   Ⓓ In an experiment, Newlands was able to prove that an element's mass and its chemical behavior were related.

4. The phrase corresponding to in the passage is closest in meaning to
   Ⓐ representing   Ⓑ equating   Ⓒ comparing   Ⓓ relating

5. According to paragraph 4, which of the following is NOT true about Dmitri Mendeleev?
   Ⓐ His periodic table left blanks for four elements.
   Ⓑ He changed the atomic numbers for certain elements.
   Ⓒ His organization of the periodic table was based on observation.
   Ⓓ He created the modern version of the periodic table.
   Paragraph 4 is marked with an arrow [➡].

6. The word their in the passage refers to

   (A) physicists   (B) X-rays   (C) elements   (D) noble gases

7. **Directions:** Complete the table by matching the statements below. Select the appropriate phrases from the answer choices and match them to the chemist to which they relate. TWO of the answer choices will NOT be used. *This question is worth 4 points.*

Drag your answer choices to the spaces where they belong. To remove an answer choice, click on it. To review the passage, click on **View Text**.

Answer Choices	Johannes Dobereiner
(A) He guessed an element's mass had an effect on chemical reactions.	▶ ▶
(B) He was one of the first to arrange elements according to their properties.	
(C) He assumed some elements had yet to be discovered.	**John Newlands**
(D) He suggested grouping elements in groups of three.	▶
(E) He noticed inaccuracies with the atomic masses of certain elements.	▶
(F) He placed the noble gases between the halogens and alkali metals.	**Dmitri Mendeleev**
(G) He compared the properties of elements with music.	▶
(H) He demonstrated a better way to arrange the elements according to their atomic number.	▶ ▶
(I) He published the modern form of the periodic table that we use today in 1869.	

Actual Practice Test

The Magic of Georges Méliès

→ Born in Paris, France, in 1861, Georges Méliès was a hugely influential figure in the creation of cinema and special effects. Though often overlooked in favor of the Lumière brothers, Méliès had a critical role in the development of cinema. In fact, the Lumière brothers proved to be a catalyst for the career of Méliès when in December 1895 the brothers publicly demonstrated their Cinématographe, the film projector. Méliès was captivated by the Cinématographe's magical potential and was determined to have a film projector of his own. When the Lumières refused to sell him theirs, he had a similar machine built, which came to be known as the kinetograph. Whereas the Lumière brothers concentrated on producing short films rooted in realism and their vision of an orderly universe, Méliès specialized in fantastic, magical stories using special effects.

Méliès started his career in entertainment by appearing as an illusionist at a number of Parisian venues, including the Cabinet Fantastique, while at the same time developing a keen interest in photography. In 1888, he purchased the Theater Robert-Houdin in Paris, where he refined his skills as a performer, designer, and producer while staging magic shows. He would go on to use many of the tricks he developed during this time in his films.

→ Méliès created his first film with his kinetograph camera in 1896 and screened it to an enthralled audience at the Robert-Houdin, and later that year a happy accident occurred that has since become legend. ■ While filming an everyday street scene, the camera Méliès was using jammed, and he had to spend a few moments fixing it before he could restart filming. ■ Later on when he processed the film, he noticed that objects suddenly appeared, disappeared, or were transformed into other objects. ■ Through this fortunate occurrence, Méliès recognized that not only could his kinetograph be used to record magic but also that magic could be created within the camera itself. ■

With his newfound skill for manipulating and distorting time and space, Méliès went on to develop a series of complex special effects, pioneering the first double exposure and the first split-screen shot with actors performing more than one part in the same scene, as well as tricks such as slow motion and fade-out. By 1901, Méliès was way ahead of his American counterparts, utilizing editing to improve special effects. In his 1901 film *The Man with the Rubber Head*, Méliès employed specially built platforms to create the illusion of enlarging objects. He went on to construct sophisticated models, such as an exploding volcano in *The Eruption of Mount Pelee* (1902). In *A Trip to the Moon* (1902), his best-known science-fiction film, by combining stage tricks, camera tricks, and a number of animation types, he used a cannon to shoot a spaceship into the eye of a face he had created in the moon. In some of his other works, he sliced people in two and transformed humans into beasts. Through these techniques, Méliès laid the foundations for countless special effects that are now taken for granted and can still be seen in modern blockbusters.

1. According to paragraph 1, the Lumière brothers affected Méliès by
   A supporting his first film productions
   B exposing him to early special effects
   C sharing their design for a film projector
   D inspiring him to create his own film projector
   Paragraph 1 is marked with an arrow [➡].

2. Why does the author mention realism and the concept of an orderly universe in paragraph 1?
   A To contrast the specialty of the Lumière brothers with that of Méliès
   B To suggest that Méliès borrowed many of the Lumière brothers' ideas
   C To give an example of the subjects Méliès favored
   D To explain how Méliès's early career influenced his later films
   Paragraph 1 is marked with an arrow [➡].

3. Why does the author mention the Theater Robert-Houdin?
   A To discuss where Méliès showed his films to the public
   B To compare it to the Cabinet Fantastique
   C To explain how Méliès was able to develop his skills
   D To identify a venue for magicians in Paris

4. The word enthralled in the passage is closest in meaning to
   A disappointed   B curious
   C fascinated   D ordinary

5. How does the author describe Méliès's discovery of special effects in paragraph 3?
   A By telling the history of his trials and errors
   B By detailing the scientific procedure he used
   C By identifying the film in which they appeared
   D By explaining the event that led to it
   Paragraph 3 is marked with an arrow [➡].

6. The word distorting in the passage is closest in meaning to

   Ⓐ changing   Ⓑ limiting

   Ⓒ saving   Ⓓ holding

7. Which of the sentences below best expresses the essential information in the highlighted sentence in the passage? *Incorrect* choices change the meaning in important ways or leave out essential information.

   Ⓐ Using a number of techniques, Méliès's famous *A Trip to the Moon* featured a spaceship being shot into the moon's eye.

   Ⓑ A science-fiction film made by Georges Méliès became very popular due to its depiction of space travel to the moon.

   Ⓒ With a memorable scene in which a cannon fires a ship into the moon, *A Trip to the Moon* is one of Méliès's classics.

   Ⓓ Various stage and camera tricks, as well as animation, were used in the production of *A Trip to the Moon*.

8. Georges Méliès is credited with the invention of all of the following EXCEPT

   Ⓐ the slow-motion effect

   Ⓑ animation technique

   Ⓒ the double exposure shot

   Ⓓ the split-screen shot

9. Look at the four squares [■] that indicate where the following sentence could be added to the passage.

    In one instance, a horse-drawn carriage disappeared and seemed to reappear as a hearse.

Where would the sentence best fit?

        Click on a square [■] to add the sentence to the passage.

10. **Directions:** An introductory sentence for a brief summary of the passage is provided below. Complete the summary by selecting the THREE answer choices that express the most important ideas in the passage. Some sentences do not belong in the summary because they express ideas that are not presented in the passage or are minor ideas in the passage. ***This question is worth 2 points.***

> Georges Méliès played a huge role in the development of cinema in the late nineteenth and early twentieth centuries.
>
> •
>
> •
>
> •

Answer Choices

(A) Méliès's encounter with the Lumières' Cinématographe in 1895 was an important moment in his life.

(B) Méliès stumbled upon his camera's ability to create illusions following a random accident during filming.

(C) *The Man with the Rubber Head* and *A Trip to the Moon* are two of Méliès's most celebrated works.

(D) Beginning his career as a magician, Méliès had a film projector made after seeing one in action.

(E) Méliès perfected his various performance skills in the Theater Robert-Houdin.

(F) The techniques pioneered by Méliès in his many films changed the cinematic world, and their effects are still evident today.

> Drag your answer choices to the spaces where they belong. To remove an answer choice, click on it. To review the passage, click on **View Text**.

Organization

The Magic of Georges Méliès

Beginning of Georges Méliès's filmmaking
- inspired by the _____ _____ created by the Lumière brothers
- focused on fantastic, magical stories employing _____ _____

Early career as a stage magician
- began his career as an illusionist
- purchased the _____ _____ as a venue to stage his shows

A crucial _____ in the development of filmmaking
- his camera _____ during the filming of a street scene
- the resulting film showed him the potential to create special effects on films

Special effects of Méliès
- created _____ exposure, split screens, _____ motion, and fade-out
- best-known film was *A Trip to the Moon*, filmed in 1902
- was a major influence on modern special effects

Vocabulary Review

A **Fill in the blanks with the best answer. Change the form if necessary.**

discard	hock	intact	vague	slant	manipulate	hail

1. His handwriting in the letter is _____ a little to the left.
2. Tourists always stop by this restaurant to get a taste of its _____ of lamb.
3. The picture was very old and the original color had faded into _____ shades.
4. Archaeologists were amazed to find that the ancient cup was perfectly _____.
5. As it is impossible to _____ radioactive wastes completely, managing permanent disposal sites is critical.
6. In the science-fiction movie, the dark force was determined to _____ the main character's mind.

B **Choose the word that is closest in meaning to each highlighted word.**

1. Garlic and olive oil are the key ingredients of this wonderful pasta recipe.
   - Ⓐ products   Ⓑ constituents   Ⓒ herbs   Ⓓ methods

2. Some people used to adorn themselves with powder, wigs, feathers, and scents.
   - Ⓐ heighten   Ⓑ coordinate   Ⓒ satisfy   Ⓓ decorate

3. The traveler remembered the storekeeper's instructions to keep driving due west.
   - Ⓐ straight   Ⓑ slightly   Ⓒ opposite   Ⓓ far

4. Students who arrive late to class tend to show the same pattern in behaviors.
   - Ⓐ source   Ⓑ arrangement   Ⓒ result   Ⓓ excuse

5. By chance, Susan caught a mistake that everyone else had overlooked.
   - Ⓐ emphasized   Ⓑ favored   Ⓒ missed   Ⓓ hold

6. When she was asked to describe her lost item, she said that it was spherical, blue, and heavy.
   - Ⓐ large   Ⓑ cylindrical   Ⓒ round   Ⓓ unique

7. The assassination of Archduke Ferdinand was a major catalyst in the First World War.
   - Ⓐ focus   Ⓑ reaction   Ⓒ solution   Ⓓ accelerator

C **Choose the correct word in each sentence.**

1. A good (protector, projector) is always a part of a successful presentation.
2. Many people are (speculating, specializing) that the mayor is guilty of bribery.
3. The amount of (precipitation, perception) increased so much in the southern states that there was extreme flooding.

Sentence Simplification

Vocabulary Preview

A **Choose the word that best matches each definition.**

> (A) hesitant   (B) nurture   (C) static
>
> (D) concentric   (E) estimate   (F) unveil

1. to make known or reveal for the first time: _____
2. fixed in position; not having any movement: _____
3. appearing unsure or unwilling about an activity: _____
4. to support and help develop; to provide training for: _____
5. to approximately judge a thing's value, size, or nature: _____

B **Choose the best synonym for each list of words.**

> (A) fragment   (B) turbulent   (C) assess   (D) substitute
>
> (E) widespread   (F) viable   (G) split

1. common   popular   general   : _____
2. evaluate   rate   judge   : _____
3. divide   separate   part   : _____
4. violent   stormy   furious   : _____
5. workable   practical   applicable : _____
6. replace   exchange   switch   : _____

C **Choose the right meaning for each highlighted word.**

1. Unmanned vehicles are often used for deep space or ocean exploration.
   (A) not having a human on board   (B) researched and proven to be good

2. The themes and images in the book manifest the author's unique style and humor.
   (A) to show something clearly   (B) to make more attractive

3. The length of her essay was substantially shortened after the final changes.
   (A) from a logical point of view   (B) significantly in amount

4. In the movie, the two main characters are forced to embark on a difficult journey.
   (A) to begin   (B) to continue to suffer through

5. His views on the country's health-care system changed radically after his visit to the inner city.
   (A) in a considerably different manner   (B) in a way that is extremely advantageous

Sentence Simplification

Introduction

- Sentence Simplification questions require you to find the best paraphrasing of the most important ideas in a long and complicated sentence from the passage.
- The original sentence is highlighted within the passage.
- 0 to 1 questions are given for each passage.

Question Type

Which of the sentences below best expresses the essential information in the highlighted sentence in the passage? *Incorrect* choices change the meaning in important ways or leave out essential information.

Strategy

1. Eliminate secondary information to identify the main idea. Information such as the following is most likely to be secondary.
   ① Information in relative clauses – these are phrases that often start with *which*, *that*, etc.
   ② Information providing an example – this type of information often comes after words like *such as*, *for example*, *like*, etc.
   ③ Information that demonstrates equivalence – these often come after dashes (–), commas (,), etc.

2. Choose the answer that correctly paraphrases the highlighted sentence. Common ways to paraphrase include:
   ① Employing different but similar words or phrases
   ② Transforming a complex sentence into a simple one
   ③ Using a different transition word to change sentence order

Basic Drills

The scientific method of evaluating human exposures to natural and synthetic compounds in the environment based on analysis of human tissues and fluids is known as biomonitoring. Blood, urine, breast milk, and expelled air are the most commonly employed measurements, but hair, nails, fat, and bone are also used. This technique allows scientists to directly assess if people have been exposed to particular substances, the amount of their exposures, and how these exposures alter over time. It takes advantage of the knowledge that chemicals that have entered the human body leave markers reflecting this exposure. The marker may take the form of the actual chemical, manifest itself as a partial form of the chemical, or reveal some change in the body resulting from the effect of the chemical on a person. The results of biomonitoring are used to aid with research into sources of human exposures, as well as to assess possible health effects.

1 Which of the sentences below best expresses the essential information in the highlighted sentence in the passage?

Ⓐ Biomonitoring data is used in managing the health risks of chemicals.

Ⓑ The findings of biomonitoring help us to analyze the consequences of past exposures.

Ⓒ Biomonitoring enables us to prevent human exposures in the future.

Ⓓ The findings of biomonitoring help us to understand human exposures and their influence on health.

Cubism was a completely new style of painting created by Pablo Picasso and Georges Braque between 1907 and 1914. Cubist painters went against the traditional concept that art should copy nature. Instead, they fragmented objects to depict a radically new style of painting where several sides of an object could be viewed at once. One famous example of this style was Picasso's *Girl with Dark Hair*, which showed the front and side of a face at the same time. In this work, Picasso illustrated the way in which space could be cut up, distorted, and altered into different planes and vistas. The Cubist painters attempted to show that people do not view things from one static, all-encompassing location, but rather from a countless number of glances that are assembled in the viewer's mind into one complete picture.

2 Which of the sentences below best expresses the essential information in the highlighted sentence in the passage?

Ⓐ Cubism shows that people do not stand in only one place when examining an abstract piece of artwork.

Ⓑ Cubism represents a style of art that can be understood only when the viewer looks at artwork several times.

Ⓒ Cubism allows viewers to look at all sides of the artwork from different points of view.

Ⓓ Cubism illustrates that viewers understand a picture by looking at it from many perspectives as opposed to one particular viewpoint.

Reading Practice 01

Scientists did not know a lot about Neptune until NASA's unmanned spacecraft Voyager 2 traveled 2.6 billion miles across space and passed the planet in 1989. Neptune is a gas giant, about four times bigger than the earth, with a small solid core and an outer atmosphere made up mostly of hydrogen and helium. It is believed that deep within Neptune's atmosphere there exists a very different inner atmosphere, a turbulent mix of molten rock, ammonia, water, and methane ⁵ that encircles the planet's core and is subject to extreme pressure and heat.

Based on what is known about Neptune, some astronomers believe that its atmospheric conditions, combined with its chemical composition, may actually be responsible for the creation of giant diamonds. The composition of Neptune's atmosphere is estimated to be about 15 percent methane, which is the key to the diamond hypothesis. A carbon atom in the middle surrounded ¹⁰ by four hydrogen atoms at its corners makes up one methane molecule (CH_4). When temperature and pressure are sufficiently high, this molecule can separate into hydrogen and carbon, with the separated carbon atoms being able to compress into diamond. Neptune's extreme heat, which can get as high as 13,000°F due to high pressure forming extremely hot gases, can split methane molecules, allowing the carbon atoms to attach directly to one another, while the pressure ¹⁵ compresses them into diamond crystals. If this phenomenon is indeed occurring on Neptune, the result would be great quantities of hydrogen gas being released into the outer atmosphere, with solid diamonds dropping down onto the planet's surface.

1   Which of the sentences below best expresses the essential information in the first highlighted sentence in paragraph 2? *Incorrect* choices change the meaning in important ways or leave out essential information.

A Studies of Neptune have shown that its chemical makeup may permit giant diamonds to exist in its atmosphere.

B The giant diamonds on Neptune prove that diamonds can be created in specific atmospheric and chemical conditions.

C The atmospheric and chemical conditions on Neptune may facilitate the creation of giant diamonds.

D Because of the presence of giant diamonds on Neptune, scientists can deduce the planet's chemical and atmospheric conditions.

2   Which of the sentences below best expresses the essential information in the second highlighted sentence in paragraph 2? *Incorrect* choices change the meaning in important ways or leave out essential information.

A Because of Neptune's extreme heat and pressure, carbon atoms from broken methane molecules can come together and condense into diamond crystals.

B Carbon atoms attach to methane molecules to form diamond crystals when temperatures and pressure are high enough.

C Due to the hot gases prevalent on Neptune, diamond crystals can form and combine into gigantic sizes.

D Because Neptune's temperatures can reach up to 13,000°F, the carbon atoms in its atmosphere are combined to create diamonds.

Summary

_____ is a gas giant whose atmospheric conditions and chemical makeup might be responsible for the creation of _____. The planet's inner atmosphere consists of a combination of methane and other elements. Because the _____ contents of the atmosphere experience very high levels of heat and _____, they can separate into hydrogen and carbon atoms, and _____ _____ might be able to join together and compress into huge diamonds.

When visible light travels from one substance into another, the light waves may experience a phenomenon called refraction, which involves the light bending or changing its direction. In the latter part of the seventeenth century, Sir Isaac Newton carried out a number of experiments dealing with the refraction of light that resulted in his discovery of the visible light spectrum. Newton situated a glass prism in front of a narrow ray of sunlight coming from a hole made in a 5 window shutter inside a darkened room. An ordered spectrum of color could be witnessed being projected onto a screen behind the prism when the sunlight passed through the prism. This experiment allowed Newton to demonstrate that white light is composed of a series of colors: red, orange, yellow, green, blue, and violet.

Furthermore, Newton revealed that the color spectrum could refract the white light 10 back together. By placing a second prism nearby the first, Newton showed that when all of the dispersed colors traveled through the second prism, they combined again into white light. This was conclusive evidence that white light is made up of a spectrum of colors that can easily be divided and reunited.

Upon conducting further experiments, Newton found that when light passed through a lens, 15 a similar thing happened as to when light traveled through the prism, leading to images being surrounded by a spectrum of colors. It occurred to him that any refracting telescope that employs lenses would have trouble getting a more accurate focus of objects due to central images in refracting telescopes being surrounded by different-colored rings. To solve this problem, Newton constructed a telescope in 1671 that employed mirrors instead of lenses to bring the light to a 20 focus. He was able to substantially reduce the length of a telescope by using a curved mirror to reflect and focus the light inside the tube, thus creating a clearer vision.

1 Which of the sentences below best expresses the essential information in the highlighted sentence in paragraph 2? *Incorrect* choices change the meaning in important ways or leave out essential information.

(A) Newton revealed that two prisms placed next to each other could disperse and combine colors at the same time.

(B) According to Newton, with two prisms, a variety of colors could be joined to create white light.

(C) When placed adjacent to each other, two prisms could cause white light to disperse into a variety of colors.

(D) Newton demonstrated that separated colors could be joined together again into white light by placing two prisms close to each other.

2 Which of the sentences below best expresses the essential information in the highlighted sentence in paragraph 3? *Incorrect* choices change the meaning in important ways or leave out essential information.

(A) He found that in order to achieve a more accurate focus, refracting telescopes needed to use lenses that did not contain different-colored rings.

(B) He discovered that it was not possible to get an accurate focus of objects with a refracting telescope.

(C) He understood that refracting telescopes caused rings of different colors to appear around objects where there was not an accurate focus.

(D) He realized that rings of different color surrounded central images in refracting telescopes with lenses, which could therefore not achieve a more accurate focus of objects.

Organization

- The _____ of light — the action of bending or changing the _____ of light waves
- Newton's experiment —— used two glass prisms
  - white light can be dispersed into an ordered color spectrum
  - dispersed colors can combine again into _____ _____
- Newton's telescope —— used curved _____ instead of _____
  - created a(n) _____ _____ of objects

● iBT Practice 01

The Daguerreotype Process

Unveiled to the world at a meeting of the French Academy of Sciences in Paris on August 19, 1839, the daguerreotype process was the first practical method of obtaining permanent images with a camera. It was able to capture very fine, rich details that offered a mirror image of the original scene and seemed to possess three dimensions. The daguerreotype was the Polaroid of its time, producing a single image which was not reproducible.   5

➡ Louis Jacques Mandé Daguerre, a French artist, perfected this method. In 1829, he forged a partnership with Joseph Nicéphore Niépce, a French amateur scientist and inventor who had succeeded in securing a picture of the view from his window by using a camera obscura and pewter plate in 1826. Niépce named his picture-making process heliography and was able to produce the world's first permanent photograph using it. However, his process was not   10 commercially feasible because of the lengthy exposure time it required – the subject and camera had to remain motionless for up to 8 hours to form the image.

Following Niépce's death in 1833, Daguerre continued to experiment on his own in search of an improved method to produce images with a camera. By 1837, he had finalized a process based on heliography and claimed the invention of "the daguerreotype" as his own. Daguerre's   15 process replaced Niépce's pewter plate and resin with silver-plated copper sheets and iodine, and he also employed warm mercury vapor to drastically reduce the exposure time of his photographic images from a number of hours to twenty to thirty minutes.

➡ The American public quickly seized on the opportunity to produce a "truthful likeness" of an image with a relatively short exposure time. Various improvements completed within a year   20 of the invention's initial disclosure further shortened the required exposure time to mere seconds, ensuring that the daguerreotype would become the first commercially viable photographic process. Before long, a profitable market for daguerreotype portraiture arose, and by 1850 there were over 70 daguerreotype studios in New York City. However, after enjoying ten years of widespread use, the popularity of the daguerreotype declined in the late 1850s upon the   25 introduction of the ambrotype, a faster and less expensive photographic process.

Glossary

camera obscura: a dark boxlike device with a small hole in one side, through which images of outside objects are projected onto an opposing wall or screen

1. Why does the author mention Polaroid?
   (A) To describe the influence the daguerreotype had on later inventions
   (B) To compare the daguerreotype to a familiar, modern product
   (C) To suggest that the daguerreotype process is still in use today
   (D) To emphasize the shortcomings of the daguerreotype process

2. According to paragraph 2, the main limitation of heliography was
   (A) the dangerous risks posed by the materials used
   (B) the too-long exposure time required to produce an image
   (C) the complicated process of developing an image
   (D) its use of the expensive camera obscura
   Paragraph 2 is marked with an arrow [➡].

3. Which of the sentences below best expresses the essential information in the highlighted sentence in the passage? *Incorrect* choices change the meaning in important ways or leave out essential information.
   (A) Daguerre was successful in his attempt to reduce the exposure time of Niépce's process from several hours to just twenty to thirty minutes.
   (B) Daguerre's process made use of silver-plated copper sheets and iodine instead of a pewter plate and resin.
   (C) Silver-plated copper, iodine, and mercury vapor allowed Daguerre to imitate the method of image production achieved by Niépce.
   (D) By substituting new materials for several components of Niépce's process, Daguerre made improvements in the length of exposure time.

4. The word disclosure in the passage is closest in meaning to
   (A) discovery   (B) projection   (C) revision   (D) announcement

5. The word viable in the passage is closest in meaning to
   (A) famous   (B) outstanding   (C) practical   (D) popular

6. It can be inferred from paragraph 4 that many people in New York City around 1850 were interested in

    Ⓐ having their portraits drawn by artists

    Ⓑ having their pictures taken by the daguerreotype process

    Ⓒ improving the daguerreotype process

    Ⓓ replacing the daguerreotype with the ambrotype

Paragraph 4 is marked with an arrow [➝].

7. **Directions:** An introductory sentence for a brief summary of the passage is provided below. Complete the summary by selecting the THREE answer choices that express the most important ideas in the passage. Some sentences do not belong in the summary because they express ideas that are not presented in the passage or are minor ideas in the passage. ***This question is worth 2 points.***

> In 1839, the daguerreotype process became the first realistic means by which to produce a photographic copy of an image.
>
> •
>
> •
>
> •

Answer Choices

    Ⓐ Daguerre introduced his revolutionary new invention to the French Academy of Sciences in Paris, where it was well received.

    Ⓑ Daguerre worked with the inventor Niépce, whose 1826 camera required too long an exposure time to be successful.

    Ⓒ The daguerreotype process was created when Daguerre improved upon Niépce's technique and decreased its exposure time.

    Ⓓ At first, the general public was hesitant to embrace the new photographic technology introduced by Daguerre.

    Ⓔ The 1850s saw a rapid rise in the popularity of the daguerreotype process but also the start of its decline.

    Ⓕ The ambrotype photographic process was more efficient in both time and cost than the daguerreotype process.

Drag your answer choices to the spaces where they belong. To remove an answer choice, click on it. To review the passage, click on **View Text**.

iBT Practice 02

PART A

UNIT 04 SENTENCE SIMPLIFICATION

A New Deal for the Arts

In the aftermath of the Great Depression, the 1930s were a time of economic gloom for the American people. President Franklin Delano Roosevelt set up New Deal cultural programs in 1935 to provide economic relief and cultural enrichment to all its citizens. The federal cultural programs of the 1930s were based on concern for tens of thousands of artists who had lost their livelihoods due to the state of the economy and the skyrocketing popularity of media like the phonograph, radio, and movies. Of the New Deal cultural programs, the largest and most important was the Works Progress Administration (WPA), a huge back-to-work program launched in the spring of 1935 to provide tax dollars to artists, musicians, actors, writers, photographers, and dancers.

➡ The WPA arts projects were known as Federal One. Federal One's philosophy was to provide jobs for the unemployed that would be beneficial for the public and conserve the skills and self-esteem of workers throughout the U.S. In particular, young men and women who were embarking on a career in the arts during the Great Depression were to be nurtured. The projects comprised four major divisions: FAP, FTP, FMP, and FWP.

The Federal Art Project (FAP) commissioned painters and sculptors to create works of art and teach art history classes. At its peak in 1936, the FAP employed 5,300 visual artists and related professionals to produce murals, paintings, sculptures, and other artistic ventures for public consumption.

The Federal Theatre Project (FTP) was created as a "free, adult, uncensored" federal theater and presented more than 1,000 performances each month to almost one million people; 78% of these audience members were not charged, many seeing live theater for the first time.

Meanwhile, the Federal Music Project (FMP) employed approximately 16,000 performers – orchestras and chamber groups; choral and opera units; concert, military and dance bands; and theater orchestras – and presented an estimated 5,000 performances before three million people every week.

The Federal Writers Project (FWP) employed 6,686 writers at the height of its operation in April 1936 to produce a variety of publications. It is best-known for its *American Guide Series*, intended to produce comprehensive guidebooks for every state in the U.S.

➡ By employing 3.5 million persons in more than 1,000 cities, the WPA helped foster a distinctly American art. However, because total federal appropriations for the program came to $11 billion, officials were very critical and argued that money was being wasted on unnecessary projects. In 1939, certain WPA projects were canceled and federal funding was reduced. After Roosevelt finally signed the order to bring it to an end, the WPA finished on June 30, 1943.

1. The word enrichment in the passage is closest in meaning to
   Ⓐ activity   Ⓑ improvement   Ⓒ heritage   Ⓓ exchange

2. Which of the sentences below best expresses the essential information in the highlighted
   sentence in the passage? *Incorrect* choices change the meaning in important ways or leave out
   essential information.
   Ⓐ Government cultural programs of the 1930s tried to help artists struggling due to the bad
      economy and arrival of new types of media.
   Ⓑ The 1930s saw the formation of cultural programs aimed at blocking the negative aspects
      of popular new media.
   Ⓒ The cultural programs of the 1930s were launched to revive the economy and improve the
      quality of life of artists.
   Ⓓ The lack of commercial support for the arts led the government to set up federal cultural
      programs in the 1930s.

3. According to paragraph 2, which of the following is NOT mentioned as an aim of Federal One?
   Ⓐ Preserving the self-respect of American workers
   Ⓑ Increasing access to the arts for people with low incomes
   Ⓒ Providing jobs for the unemployed
   Ⓓ Nurturing young adults who are beginning their careers
   Paragraph 2 is marked with an arrow [➡].

4. The word commissioned in the passage is closest in meaning to
   Ⓐ helped   Ⓑ appointed   Ⓒ ordered   Ⓓ convinced

5. According to paragraph 7, the WPA finished in 1943 because
   Ⓐ there were not enough talented artists to carry out its work
   Ⓑ the economy had improved enough to make the WPA unnecessary
   Ⓒ government officials felt money was being wasted on unworthy projects
   Ⓓ there was not enough federal money left to maintain the programs
   Paragraph 7 is marked with an arrow [➡].

6. According to the passage, which of the following is true of the WPA arts projects?

    (A) The FAP employed more than 5,000 artists and provided them with a weekly wage.

    (B) The FTP provided free movies for all American cinemagoers.

    (C) The FMP gave up to 5,000 performances every month to the American public.

    (D) The FWP produced a series of guidebooks covering all of the American states.

7. **Directions:** An introductory sentence for a brief summary of the passage is provided below. Complete the summary by selecting the THREE answer choices that express the most important ideas in the passage. Some sentences do not belong in the summary because they express ideas that are not presented in the passage or are minor ideas in the passage. ***This question is worth 2 points.***

> In the 1930s, President Roosevelt introduced a number of cultural programs that became known as Federal One.
>
> -
> -
> -

Answer Choices

    (A) Federal One was established within the WPA as a central administration for arts-related projects.

    (B) Federal One collected taxes from workers in the artistic fields to promote cultural activities.

    (C) Despite its contribution to the arts, Federal One was reduced in scale and finally stopped because of criticism by officials.

    (D) Federal One instituted cultural programs to help the unemployed in the fields of art, music, theater, and writing.

    (E) The four major projects of Federal One provided the public with various educational opportunities.

    (F) Federal One's target was to provide jobs for out-of-work artists and give support to newcomers to the arts.

Drag your answer choices to the spaces where they belong. To remove an answer choice, click on it. To review the passage, click on **View Text**.

Actual Practice Test

Burgess's Concentric Zone Theory

Ernest W. Burgess was an urban sociologist at the University of Chicago who gave birth to the theory of urban ecology, a branch of ecology that analyzes the relationship between humans and their environments in urban or urbanizing settings. As a member of the so-called Chicago School of scholars working at the University of Chicago, Burgess focused on the form and development of the modern American city and tried to find out how the sociological, psychological, and moral 5 aspects of urban living were reflected in spatial relationships.

➡ In 1924, Burgess presented the famous concentric zone theory, which was based on his observations of Chicago during the early years of the twentieth century. He believed that the accessibility of a central location made it the most valuable part of a city, and hence it becomes an important employment center within a city. He also claimed that low-income households prefer 10 to live in close proximity to their workplaces, whereas richer people prefer to live closer to the natural environment. Based on the interests of a particular group, areas spread in concentric zones outward from the center of a city.

➡ In a definitive manner, he identified the concentric zones from the more expensive land of the central business district (CBD) in the center through five distinct zones. Zone 1 was the 15 CBD itself, the economic and geographical center of the city, where consumer and commercial activities were focused. ■ The outer areas of this zone had lower rents and contained warehouses, storage facilities, and the wholesale business district. ■ Zone 2 was labeled the transition zone and included older factories and an area of deteriorating neighborhoods where immigrants usually resided in cheap housing; this zone was associated with high crime rates and social 20 disorganization. ■ Zone 3 was the residential area typically settled by blue-collar workers and second-generation immigrants who had moved out from Zone 2. ■ After this area came Zone 4, the outer city area of the middle class, characterized by small business owners, professional people, and white-collar workers. Finally there was Zone 5, the "commuter zone" or suburbs comprising of the upper-middle-class and classic suburban lifestyles of comfortable living and leisure. 25

He proposed that the expansion and formation of these concentric zones are a result of processes called invasion and succession. Over time, as a city grows and develops, the CBD puts pressure on the zone immediately surrounding it, known as the zone of transition. As the CBD grows outward, it would invade nearby residential neighborhoods forcing them to expand outward. This process was believed to continue, with each successive neighborhood moving 30 further away from the CBD. As a city grows and its CBD expands outward, lower-status residents move to bordering neighborhoods and richer residents move further away from the CBD because inner city housing is mostly occupied by immigrants and households with low socio-economic status.

➡ Burgess's model has come in for criticism from various observers. It has been accused ₃₅ of being too simple, only applicable to social and cultural conditions in cities up to the 1950s, and inappropriate as a method of understanding modern cities. Furthermore, the concentric model was developed with American cities in mind and clearly did not fit the evolution of most European cities. Nevertheless, it has still become one of the most prominent theories of urban sociology and serves as a useful way to explain urban land use and urban growth in early twentieth- ₄₀ century American cities. It has also been extensively used to explain social problems such as unemployment and crime in certain areas of cities.

1.   Which of the sentences below best expresses the essential information in the highlighted sentence in the passage? *Incorrect* choices change the meaning in important ways or leave out essential information.
   Ⓐ From his viewpoint as a member of the Chicago School, Burgess analyzed how various aspects of urban living affected the form and progression of American cities.
   Ⓑ Burgess used his experience as a member of the Chicago School to examine the various aspects of urban life in modern American cities.
   Ⓒ By studying the development of American cities, Burgess was able to understand the social, moral, and psychological traits of urban dwellers in the U.S.
   Ⓓ As a member of the Chicago School, Burgess tried to find out how the modern American city had been developed.

2.   Paragraph 2 suggests that the center of a city became most valuable because
   Ⓐ it contains an important employment center
   Ⓑ it is the most accessible place in a city
   Ⓒ it is near the shopping district
   Ⓓ it has a lot of convenient facilities
   Paragraph 2 is marked with an arrow [➡].

3.   According to paragraph 3, which of the following is true about the five distinct zones of a city?
   Ⓐ Zone 2 included storage and warehouse facilities for CBD businesses.
   Ⓑ Zone 3 was mostly home to white-collar workers and second-generation immigrants.
   Ⓒ Zone 4 contained small-sized business owners and professional people.
   Ⓓ Zone 5 provided comfortable living conditions for both the rich and poor.
   Paragraph 3 is marked with an arrow [➡].

4. In paragraph 3, in what order does the author explain a series of concentric zones?
    Ⓐ From the most expensive zone to the cheapest one
    Ⓑ From residential areas to business districts
    Ⓒ From the inner area to the outer area of a city
    Ⓓ From white-collar areas to blue-collar neighborhoods
    Paragraph 3 is marked with an arrow [➡].

5. The word it in the passage refers to
    Ⓐ city   Ⓑ CBD   Ⓒ pressure   Ⓓ zone of transition

6. Why does the author mention European cities?
    Ⓐ To contrast American cities with European cities
    Ⓑ To explain why the concentric zone model became so famous
    Ⓒ To illustrate another application of the concentric zone model
    Ⓓ To demonstrate a weakness of the concentric zone theory

7. The word prominent in the passage is closest in meaning to
    Ⓐ questionable   Ⓑ famous   Ⓒ academic   Ⓓ accurate

8. What can be inferred from paragraph 5 about cities in America after the 1950s?
    Ⓐ They were similar to European cities in developmental aspects at the time.
    Ⓑ They were more modern than European cities at the time.
    Ⓒ They contained different types of residents compared to pre-1950s cities.
    Ⓓ They demonstrated different developmental aspects from pre-1950s cities.
    Paragraph 5 is marked with an arrow [➡].

9. Look at the four squares [■] that indicate where the following sentence could be added to the passage.

    Major department stores, theaters, hotels, and banks tended to be located in this zone.

    Where would the sentence best fit?

    Click on a square [■] to add the sentence to the passage.

10. **Directions:** An introductory sentence for a brief summary of the passage is provided below. Complete the summary by selecting the THREE answer choices that express the most important ideas in the passage. Some sentences do not belong in the summary because they express ideas that are not presented in the passage or are minor ideas in the passage. ***This question is worth 2 points.***

> Through his concentric zone model, E. W. Burgess examined how the relationship between humans and their surroundings affected the evolution of American cities.
>
> -
> -
> -

Answer Choices

Ⓐ Burgess was the first scholar to examine the effects of people's relationships with their environments on the development of urban areas.

Ⓑ Using Chicago as his model, Burgess suggested that a city grows outward from its center in a set of concentric zones with each zone devoted to different land use.

Ⓒ Burgess proposed that upper-class residents choose to live in the suburbs, while poorer people are forced to live in the center of a city.

Ⓓ Burgess's model has been widely used to explain social problems in certain areas of a city.

Ⓔ Burgess claimed that the expansion of zones was caused by a growing central business district forcing each zone to successively grow outward away from the center.

Ⓕ Despite its limitations, Burgess's model is considered one of the most useful explanations of urban land use in the early twentieth century.

> Drag your answer choices to the spaces where they belong. To remove an answer choice, click on it. To review the passage, click on **View Text**.

Organization

Burgess's Concentric Zone Theory

Introduction of E. W. Burgess

- developed a theory of urban ecology
- examined how spatial relationships reflected aspects of urban living
  in the _____ _____ city

The concentric zone theory

- Introduction of the theory

  - believed a(n) _____ area became the most valuable place in a city
  - different groups of people have different preferences for housing locations.

- The characteristics of 5 zones

  - Zone 1: _____ and geographical core of the city
  - Zone 2: area of cheap housing for _____
  - Zone 3: area for the residences of _____ _____
    and second-generation immigrants
  - Zone 4: home of the city's _____ _____
  - Zone 5: upscale suburbs for commuters

- The process of zone expansion

  - Zones expand outward from the CBD.
  - Richer citizens migrate away from poorer neighborhoods.

- The weakness and usefulness of the theory

  - considered an overly simple theory that does not apply to _____ cities
  - is useful in understanding the root causes of urban social issues

Vocabulary Review

A   **Fill in the blanks with the best answer. Change the form if necessary.**

skyrocket	aid	encircle	gloom	finalize	reproducible

1. The very last thing for us to do is _____ the word choice in two places.
2. The most important role of a teacher is to _____ students in learning how to think for themselves.
3. _____ and darkness can be easily found in the works of the American poet Edgar Allan Poe.
4. The high fence that _____ the prison makes it difficult for people to escape.
5. One reason for recording every detail of an experiment is to ensure that the same result is _____.

B   **Choose the word or phrase that is closest in meaning to each highlighted word.**

1. When I was young, I was labeled a troublemaker.
   - Ⓐ loved
   - Ⓑ accused
   - Ⓒ branded
   - Ⓓ misunderstood

2. They could not find any conclusive proof that Jake was guilty.
   - Ⓐ extra
   - Ⓑ decisive
   - Ⓒ adverse
   - Ⓓ formal

3. The company is known to charge fairly and to do an excellent job.
   - Ⓐ bill
   - Ⓑ hire
   - Ⓒ communicate
   - Ⓓ negotiate

4. An increase in population will most likely urbanize what used to be a rural area.
   - Ⓐ clean up
   - Ⓑ popularize
   - Ⓒ bring out
   - Ⓓ citify

5. Taking two years to work abroad before continuing school is a perfectly feasible plan.
   - Ⓐ confused
   - Ⓑ unwise
   - Ⓒ approved
   - Ⓓ possible

6. No one wanted to talk so the committee had no other option but to deduce what had happened.
   - Ⓐ explain
   - Ⓑ report
   - Ⓒ reason
   - Ⓓ question

7. Not only academic programs but art, music and sports programs also help foster students' development.
   - Ⓐ block
   - Ⓑ promote
   - Ⓒ vary
   - Ⓓ create

C   **Choose the correct word in each sentence.**

1. The two decided to (forge, surge) a team only for the purpose of winning.
2. You must always (embark, embrace) helpful advice, even when it hurts.
3. The difference in temperature causes the moisture in the warmer side to (condense, conduct) and form water drops.

PART

Making Inference

UNIT 05   INFERENCE

UNIT 06   RHETORICAL PURPOSE

UNIT

05

Inference

Vocabulary Preview

A **Choose the word that best matches each definition.**

> (A) succumb   (B) unearth   (C) impeachment
> (D) eminent   (E) jury   (F) thermal

1. a body of people chosen to listen to the facts of a case and give a verdict: _____
2. to discover something buried in the ground: _____
3. to give into an illness or die: _____
4. well known for excellence in character or performance: _____
5. a charge of misconduct made against a government official: _____

B **Choose the best synonym for each list of words.**

> (A) prestigious   (B) covet   (C) prototype   (D) deliberately
> (E) conspiracy   (F) massacre   (G) testimony

1. honored   renowned   famed   : _____
2. on purpose   intentionally   knowingly   : _____
3. evidence   statement   proof   : _____
4. plot   scheme   intrigue   : _____
5. envy   desire   hunger for   : _____
6. extermination   annihilation   wipeout   : _____

C **Choose the right meaning for each highlighted word.**

1. The star's wordy explanation for her behavior made the public suspect her even more.
   (A) to doubt someone's claims   (B) to sympathize with one's opinion

2. The centerpiece of the movie is the car chase scene, which is extremely exciting.
   (A) the most enjoyable part   (B) the most important, or central, part

3. The main effect of global warming is climatic change and its related disasters.
   (A) related to weather conditions   (B) caused by the climax of something

4. The city did its best to consolidate its efforts to rescue the hikers trapped in the mountain cabin.
   (A) to make something stronger   (B) to promise to do something

5. Coal mining was a flourishing industry before coal was replaced by other energy sources.
   (A) receiving a lot of criticism   (B) growing successfully

Inference

Introduction

- Inference questions test if you can infer an implied meaning based on information mentioned, though not obviously, in the passage.

- 0 to 2 questions are given for each passage.

Question Types

- What can be inferred from paragraph ___ about X?
- The author of the passage implies that
- In paragraph ___, the author suggests that
- It can be concluded from the information in paragraph ___ that
- According to paragraph ___, it can be inferred that
- According to paragraph ___, what does X indicate?

Strategy

In the passage, locate the key word or phrase provided in the question and carefully read both the sentence that contains it and the surrounding context. Then, based on what you understand, make inferences.

In a situation where the basis for inference is
① one sentence, quickly examine the key word/phrase and the surrounding context to locate the implied idea.
② more than one sentence, use all of the information found around the sentence that has the key word/phrase given in the question to make an inference.
③ one or more than one paragraph, locate the answer based on overall comprehension of the passage as the question commonly deals with the general theme.

Basic Drills

Correlation is a device to determine how related two variables are. There are two kinds of correlation: positive and negative. For a positive correlation, as one variable increases or decreases in value, so does the other. An example of this is when the amount of time spent in education is positively correlated with the amount of money earned. In contrast, a negative correlation occurs when one variable's value increases as the other's decreases, and vice versa — for example, when the number of people waiting for a bus goes up as the waiting time for the next bus goes down. Nevertheless, correlation does NOT imply causation in any way. In the case of time spent in education, the amount of money earned is positively correlated, but this does not mean that years spent in education determine the actual income. This is because other <u>undetected</u> factors, such as job, talent, and background, may be influencing both known variables.

1 What can be inferred about positive correlation?

(A) Additional factors which control two variables are needed.

(B) One variable's low score is associated with a second variable's low score.

(C) One variable's changes lead to another variable's changes, with no exception.

(D) When one variable's value decreases, the value of the second variable does not change.

Ancient Greek potters used the three-step firing process. During the first stage, the oxidizing stage, pottery was heated in a wood- or charcoal-fueled kiln. At the end of this firing phase, the clay would be reddish-orange because of the distinctive Athenian clay containing iron oxide. Only the parts to which the slip — diluted clay of the same material as the pot — had been applied for vase painting would have a <u>gloss</u>. In the next stage, the reducing stage, oxygen would be cut off and fresh wood would be added to provide a smoky environment, causing the entire pot to turn black. In the final stage, the re-oxidizing stage, <u>vents</u> in the kiln were opened to increase the supply of oxygen, and the kiln was gradually cooled. At this point, the clay would return to its reddish-orange color due to renewed oxidization, and only the parts where slip was applied remain black. With these three steps of the firing process, the characteristic appearance of Greek pottery was created.

2 What can be inferred about the firing process in Greek pottery?

(A) Oxygen plays a significant role in the unique coloring of Greek pottery.

(B) The control of the temperature in the kiln is crucial to the gloss of Greek pottery.

(C) The use of fresh wood affects the speed of the firing process.

(D) The use of slip in pottery was not a common practice at that time.

Vocabulary

Choose the word that is closest in meaning to the underlined word in the passage.

1. undetected	(A) unusual	(B) unsure	(C) unnoticed	(D) unimportant
2. gloss	(A) color	(B) shape	(C) shine	(D) edge
3. vents	(A) openings	(B) strings	(C) pipes	(D) corners

Reading Practice 01

→ The first Academy of Art was established in the Italian city of Florence in 1562. It was founded by Giorgio Vasari, a famed sculptor and painter. He sought to consolidate the rising social and professional status of talented artists and separate them from mere craftsmen and artisans who were looked down upon as manual laborers. This Academy served as the prototype for the prestigious Royal Academy of Painting and Sculpture, which was established in France in 1648. By 1816, it had changed its name into the Academy of Fine Arts. It recruited the most talented artists and put them through rigorous training. The intellectual aspect of art became the most important component of their study, and as a result, the subject and styles of academic art reflected this.

→ From the beginning, the mission of the French Academy was to train artists to produce work of the classical tradition. This meant aspiring artists had to adhere to the aesthetics of idealism and strive for perfection. Part of their training therefore involved studying and copying antique art such as Greek sculpture. There was also a strong emphasis on drawing and painting the nude, but the students had to endure rigorous training and prove themselves by studying plaster casts of famous classical sculptures before they were permitted to be in the presence of a live model. Likewise, a student was only given the privilege of joining the studio of a master to learn how to paint when he could prove that his drawing was good enough. During the years of training, students' progress was measured by regular competitions in which they had to produce work on a particular subject within a certain amount of time. Those who won were awarded prizes, the most coveted of which was the Prix-de-Rome. This prestigious prize allowed the winner to practice in Rome, which since 1666 had been home to a branch of the French Academy; and the winner was assured a successful professional career.

1   What can be inferred from paragraph 1 about craftsmen and artisans?
- Ⓐ They were not highly appreciated at that time.
- Ⓑ They were eager to enter the Academy of Art.
- Ⓒ They received intense training to become professional artists.
- Ⓓ They laid the foundations for the first Academy in Italy.

Paragraph 1 is marked with an arrow [➡].

2   What can be inferred from paragraph 2 about Greek sculpture?
- Ⓐ It had a religious character.
- Ⓑ It had a dramatic influence on the style of French sculpture.
- Ⓒ It was expected to represent the beauty of the human form.
- Ⓓ It represented the aesthetics of idealism and classicism.

Paragraph 2 is marked with an arrow [➡].

Extra Question

Which of the following is true about the training of the Academy?
- Ⓐ Young artists were able to study in Rome at the end of the Academy's course.
- Ⓑ Through competitions, students could choose to draw either sculptures or live models.
- Ⓒ Drawing and painting nude forms was one of the most important training modules.
- Ⓓ Copying antique art was a subject of regular competitions.

Summary

Originally founded as the Royal Academy of Painting and Sculpture in France in 1648, the Academy of Fine Arts recruited and trained the most talented artists of the age. The aim of the Academy was to nurture artists to produce work in the _____ _____, following the goals of idealism and _____. The students spent time studying _____ _____, and there was also a strong focus on drawing and painting _____ models. The students' progress was measured by _____, with the most prestigious prize being the Prix-de-Rome, which guaranteed the winner a prosperous _____.

Reading Practice 02

The word *midden* is used to describe an area where household waste is deposited. Shell middens are accumulations of shells, from shellfish such as freshwater mussels or oysters, left behind by the prehistoric humans that consumed them, often along with bones and other items. They may be buried in layers within the earth or piled up in bulging mounds. Shell middens vary greatly in size, representing anything from a single meal of a passing nomadic tribe to the accumulated waste of a civilization over thousands of years. They are usually found in flood plains or other types of wetlands, and have been unearthed by archaeologists in coastal areas all around the world.

➡ Shell middens are capable of providing valuable information on how ancient people lived, yielding evidence of what they ate, and how they prepared it. Shell middens may also contain other evidence of the culture that these people produced, such as stone tools, arrowheads, or fish hooks. Bird and animal bones found in middens can tell us what species inhabited a region in the past, while seeds can give clues to the plant life of that time. Archaeologists can also learn a variety of things from the shells themselves. Mussel shells contain growth rings that are similar to the rings found within the trunk of a tree, added at certain seasonal intervals as the organism grows. The size and shape of the rings vary according to climatic events, such as floods or droughts, giving researchers a picture of environmental conditions around the time when the shellfish were collected and consumed.

➡ Other items contained in a shell midden can be exceptionally well-preserved due to the chemical composition of the soil in which they are found. When a shell contacts groundwater in the soil, the water partially dissolves the shell, causing it to release calcium carbonate, an alkaline solution that neutralizes the soil's acidity. Because this acidity is responsible for much of the decay that occurs in bones and other organic material, neutralizing it allows any archaeological relics located in a midden to be preserved. As a result, these objects often provide extraordinary data on the lives of the ancient people who created the midden.

5

10

15

20

25

1 According to paragraph 2, it can be inferred that archaeologists study mussel shell rings in order to

    Ⓐ discover why people originally created shell middens

    Ⓑ learn about climatic conditions that ancient people faced

    Ⓒ determine the types of tools that were used to eat them

    Ⓓ compare them to tree trunk rings found in the same area

Paragraph 2 is marked with an arrow [➡].

2 What can be inferred from paragraph 3 about organic relics found in shell middens?

    Ⓐ They were damaged due to contact with groundwater.

    Ⓑ They were placed there deliberately by ancient people.

    Ⓒ They contain large amounts of calcium carbonate.

    Ⓓ They would have decayed in other locations.

Paragraph 3 is marked with an arrow [➡].

Extra Question

In paragraph 1, the author states that shell middens

    Ⓐ do not share a uniform shape and size

    Ⓑ are only found in areas close to the sea

    Ⓒ do not contain objects other than shells

    Ⓓ were usually deposited by large civilizations

Summary

_____ _____ are accumulations of shells from shellfish left behind by prehistoric people, usually in the form of layers beneath the earth or bulging mounds. Found in _____ _____ or wetland areas, middens can provide information for archaeologists about how people lived and their diets. Also, middens sometimes contain cultural evidence like stone tools the inhabitants produced, as well as _____ of animals that once lived there. Mussel shells can show _____ events of the region. The relics found in middens are well-preserved since the shells _____ the acidity of the soil, and thus archaeologists are able to gather data on the lives of ancient people.

iBT Practice 01

The Library of Alexandria

The life and death of Alexander the Great led to the establishment of probably the greatest center of learning in the ancient world, the city of Alexandria. Within two years of becoming King of Macedonia at the age of 20, Alexander had embarked on a campaign to unite the world's ancient cultures, with the centerpiece of his empire being the glorious city of Alexandria. After his death, Ptolemy I Soter inherited control of Egypt and made Alexandria his capital and seat   5 of power; and by opening the Library of Alexandria, he helped the city to become a center of learning with a profound influence on the development of knowledge.

➡ Ptolemy I set about establishing a foundation in Alexandria formerly dedicated to the Muses – the Museum of Alexandria, or Mouseion. This research institute opened its doors to the arts and sciences and contained numerous facilities for music, dance, theater, poetry, prose,   10 history, and astronomy. A key part of this complex was the Library of Alexandria, a universal storehouse of wisdom that attracted the world's most eminent scholars. Ptolemy I and his successor, Ptolemy II, used their wealth to purchase books from markets in Athens and Rhodes and their power to "borrow" books from authors, cargo ships, and other museums and libraries. All visitors to Alexandria were forced to give up their books and scrolls, which in turn were expertly   15 copied, with the originals sometimes going to the Library and the copies to the unsuspecting previous owners.

This process created a reservoir of books, with the Library containing between 500,000 and 700,000 papyrus scrolls of the most profound history and philosophy. During its golden age, the Alexandrian Library fostered important advancements in the fields of science, astronomy, and   20 medicine, with household names such as Archimedes and Euclid blossoming in its presence. For almost three centuries, the city and Library of Alexandria was the meeting place where philosophical, spiritual, and cosmological teachings combined to create a flourishing cultural environment.

➡ In 47 BC, however, the Roman legions of Julius Caesar carelessly damaged the Library,   25 and its destruction was completed in the civil war of the late third century. The destruction of the magnificent Library at Alexandria was one of the most notorious crimes of history, taking away from the world one of its greatest ever collections of literature, philosophy, and history.

1. Which of the following can be inferred from paragraph 2 about Mouseion?
   (A) It was the birthplace of modern science.
   (B) It was the world's first great academic institution.
   (C) The Library of Alexandria was founded within it.
   (D) It was a universal art institute covering all art genres.
   Paragraph 2 is marked with an arrow [➡].

2. All of the following are mentioned in paragraph 2 as contributing to the collection of books in the Library of Alexandria EXCEPT
   (A) the purchasing of books in Athenian markets
   (B) the "borrowing" of books from other libraries
   (C) the copying of books and scrolls forcibly acquired from visitors
   (D) the hiring of famous scholars to write books
   Paragraph 2 is marked with an arrow [➡].

3. The word reservoir in the passage is closest in meaning to
   (A) storage   (B) demand   (C) reproduction   (D) publication

4. Why does the author mention Archimedes and Euclid?
   (A) To provide examples of scholars that the Library fostered
   (B) To demonstrate how they contributed to the establishment of the Library
   (C) To show that they played an important role in the field of science
   (D) To show that Ptolemy I was a man of learning

5. The word magnificent in the passage is closest in meaning to
   (A) invaluable   (B) central   (C) remarkable   (D) unusual

PART B

UNIT 05 INFERENCE

6. According to paragraph 4, which of the following is true of the destruction of the Library?

    Ⓐ Julius Caesar set fire to the Library in the late third century.

    Ⓑ It happened during the reign of Ptolemy I.

    Ⓒ It was completely destroyed during a civil war.

    Ⓓ Ptolemy II made great efforts to prevent it.

    Paragraph 4 is marked with an arrow [➡].

7. **Directions:** An introductory sentence for a brief summary of the passage is provided below. Complete the summary by selecting the THREE answer choices that express the most important ideas in the passage. Some sentences do not belong in the summary because they express ideas that are not presented in the passage or are minor ideas in the passage. ***This question is worth 2 points.***

    > The Library of Alexandria helped Alexandria become the focus for the development of knowledge in the ancient world.
    >
    > •
    >
    > •
    >
    > •

    Answer Choices

    Ⓐ The destruction of the Library resulted in the permanent loss of its collection of books.

    Ⓑ Both Ptolemy I and Ptolemy II used their power and influence to collect books and scrolls from many sources.

    Ⓒ The accumulation of books from many sources helped the Library to become a magnet for the arts and sciences.

    Ⓓ The Library was to prove an inspiration for the development of arts and sciences in the Renaissance period.

    Ⓔ The creation of the Library was the most important achievement in Alexander the Great's reign.

    Ⓕ For nearly three centuries, the Library provided a fertile environment for exchanges in the major fields of intellectual pursuit.

    Drag your answer choices to the spaces where they belong. To remove an answer choice, click on it. To review the passage, click on **View Text**.

● iBT Practice 02

TOEFL Reading

Surface Thermal Inversions

➡ On an average day, a measurement of atmospheric air temperatures will reveal a gradual decrease in heat as altitude increases. This is due to solar radiation from the sun's rays heating the earth's surface. In turn, the surface transfers this heat to the air directly above it. Because heat rises, this air subsequently ascends into the atmosphere, cooling off as it moves farther away from the earth. However, this situation is sometimes reversed, with temperatures increasing rather than 5 diminishing at higher altitudes. This is known as a thermal inversion. More specifically, inversions that take place in close proximity to the earth are known as surface inversions, a phenomenon of great interest to scientists due to the direct impact it can have on the quality of our air.

➡ Most often, surface inversions form as a result of the nightly cooling of air located near the ground. On calm, clear winter nights, the cooling of the earth's surface can significantly lower 10 the temperature of the air just above it. The air higher up in the atmosphere, however, retains its temperature. Without heavy winds to blend the air of different altitudes, a surface inversion may be formed. This type of event is more common in the winter due to the increased length of nights during this season, which gives the earth's surface more time to cool down and thereby heightens the chance of an inversion. 15

A surface inversion can have adverse effects on air quality. The layer of cooler air remains trapped beneath the warmer air, unable to rise past it and disperse into the atmosphere. Inversions also create a localized region of still air, stopping the development of strong winds by preventing convection, the natural process by which warmer air rises up, cools off, and drops back down to promote constant air circulation. Without wind or dispersion into the atmosphere, 20 smoke, smog, and other pollutants accumulate just above the earth's surface, causing the air we breathe to be less clean. A strong inversion that lasts for a lengthy period can create a thick haze in the motionless air and become a serious health risk. One such event killed thousands of people in London in 1952, when a large portion of the elderly population succumbed to respiratory illnesses. 25

1. The word reversed in the passage is closest in meaning to

    (A) opposite   (B) troubling   (C) irregular   (D) uncontrolled

2. According to paragraph 1, air close to the earth's surface is hottest because

    (A) thermal inversions prevent it from rising

    (B) it descends from heated regions of the atmosphere

    (C) solar radiation is most active there

    (D) it receives heat reflected off the ground

    Paragraph 1 is marked with an arrow [➡].

3. The word it in the passage refers to

    (A) the earth's surface   (B) temperature

    (C) air   (D) atmosphere

4. What can be inferred from paragraph 2 about surface inversions during daylight hours?

    (A) They make the difference in air temperatures caused by altitude more extreme.

    (B) They occur very infrequently during the winter season.

    (C) They usually weaken as the sun warms the earth's surface.

    (D) They are more prevalent when heavy winds are present.

    Paragraph 2 is marked with an arrow [➡].

5. The word adverse in the passage is closest in meaning to

    (A) unpredictable   (B) enormous   (C) negative   (D) various

6. Why does the author mention convection?

    (A) To describe a natural threat to air quality

    (B) To explain how thermal inversions affect air quality

    (C) To introduce a way to prevent surface inversions

    (D) To identify a phenomenon that strengthens thermal inversions

7. **Directions:** An introductory sentence for a brief summary of the passage is provided below. Complete the summary by selecting the THREE answer choices that express the most important ideas in the passage. Some sentences do not belong in the summary because they express ideas that are not presented in the passage or are minor ideas in the passage. *This question is worth 2 points.*

> Thermal inversions are reversals in the normal relationship between air temperature and altitude.
>
> •
>
> •
>
> •

Answer Choices

(A) By trapping a layer of air and pollutants close to the ground, surface thermal inversions can have dramatically harmful effects on air quality.

(B) Usually, surface thermal inversions occur close to the ground due to the cooling caused by long winter nights.

(C) Thousands of London residents died of lung cancer as a result of high pollution levels caused by a surface thermal inversion.

(D) Surface thermal inversions create pockets of still air that strengthen the natural convection cycle of air movement.

(E) Though surface thermal inversions are most common during the winter, they can also form at other times of year, leading to air pollution.

(F) Under normal conditions, air becomes cooler the higher into the atmosphere it rises.

> Drag your answer choices to the spaces where they belong. To remove an answer choice, click on it. To review the passage, click on **View Text**.

PART B

UNIT 05 INFERENCE

Actual Practice Test

The Watergate Scandal

The Watergate scandal was a political scandal in the United States that began in the summer of 1972 in Washington, D.C., when several burglars were arrested while attempting to break into the headquarters of the Democratic Party, located in the Watergate office complex. Reporters soon connected the burglars to Republican President Richard Nixon and his reelection committee. This crime, as well as the Nixon administration's aggressive attempts to cover it up,   5 eventually led Nixon to resign from his position in disgrace.

→ In 1972, President Richard Nixon was running for reelection at a time when Americans were deeply divided politically and when opposition to the Vietnam War was continually growing. Nixon and his advisors believed that in such an unfriendly political environment he needed to win a decisive victory in the 1972 election. As part of their forceful reelection strategy, Nixon's   10 Committee to Reelect the President hired burglars to break into the Democratic Party's offices. They stole top-secret documents and illegally wiretapped the phones. The burglars were arrested on June 17, 1972, when a security guard caught them sneaking into the offices to replace malfunctioning wiretaps. After the break-in was reported by the media, President Nixon gave a speech assuring Americans that neither he nor his campaign was involved. That November,   15 Richard Nixon won a second term in office.

→ While most voters seemed to believe that Nixon had no knowledge of the crimes that took place, other people in Washington began to suspect a larger conspiracy. The U.S. Senate established a select committee to investigate the events surrounding Watergate. This included the testimony of former administration officials. Not only did these officials describe the crimes   20 committed by the president, but they also revealed that Nixon used a recording system that automatically taped everything said in the Oval Office. Special prosecutor Archibald Cox immediately subpoenaed the recordings. Nixon fought this subpoena, citing his executive privilege to maintain confidential communications.

→ On October 20, 1973, after Archibald Cox repeatedly refused Nixon's order to drop   25 the subpoena, Nixon ordered the attorney general to fire him. Many members of the Justice Department then resigned from their jobs in protest of the president's abuse of power. These mass resignations, known as the Saturday Night Massacre, resulted in a tremendous amount of public criticism of Richard Nixon. It also motivated the House of Representatives to begin formal impeachment hearings against him. A new special prosecutor was soon appointed, and on March   30

Glossary

Oval Office: the office of the U.S. president in the White House
subpoena: a legal document ordering a person to answer questions or provide evidence to a court of law

1, 1974, a grand jury charged seven of Richard Nixon's former aides with various crimes related to the Watergate break-in. Nixon continued to resist efforts to obtain the recordings of his White House conversations until July 1974, when the Supreme Court ordered that the tapes be released to the special prosecutor.

→ On August 5, 1974, the White House released tapes containing conversations involving ³⁵ the president which proved that he took part in a criminal cover-up, obstructed justice, and abused his presidential powers. Three days later, on the evening of August 8, 1974, President Nixon resigned from the presidency in a nationally televised address. ■ After Nixon resigned, Vice President Gerald Ford became president and pardoned Nixon for any crimes he had committed. ■ Nevertheless, the Watergate scandal caused permanent damage to American ⁴⁰ political life. ■ Richard Nixon's dishonesty and his abuse of power forever deepened Americans' cynicism and distrust of their government and political system. ■

1. The word aggressive in the passage is closest in meaning to
   (A) forceful
   (B) impulsive
   (C) insensitive
   (D) judicious

2. What can be inferred from paragraph 2 about the Vietnam War?
   (A) It was fought to slow the spread of communism.
   (B) It was an issue many Americans disagreed about.
   (C) It was a foreign policy issue Republicans supported.
   (D) It was one of Nixon's few political achievements.
   Paragraph 2 is marked with an arrow [→].

3. According to paragraph 2, it can be inferred that the burglars broke into the Watergate office complex to
   (A) plant evidence that would damage the Democratic candidate
   (B) damage equipment to disrupt the Democratic campaign
   (C) gather important information about the Democratic campaign
   (D) steal money from the Democratic campaign's election fund
   Paragraph 2 is marked with an arrow [→].

PART B

UNIT 05 INFERENCE

4. The word confidential in the passage is closest in meaning to

    Ⓐ protected   Ⓑ private

    Ⓒ immune   Ⓓ censored

5. According to paragraph 3, the existence of the White House tapes is significant because

    Ⓐ they would reveal the identities of the Watergate burglars

    Ⓑ they would contain undeniable evidence of Nixon's guilt

    Ⓒ they could prove that Nixon had no knowledge of the break-in

    Ⓓ they justified the House of Representative's impeachment inquiry

Paragraph 3 is marked with an arrow [➡].

6. The word It in the passage refers to

    Ⓐ Watergate break-in   Ⓑ subpoena of recordings

    Ⓒ Saturday Night Massacre   Ⓓ public criticism of Richard Nixon

7. In paragraph 4, why does the author mention that a new special prosecutor was appointed?

    Ⓐ To indicate that the firing of Cox did not end the investigations into the Watergate break-ins

    Ⓑ To show how determined the public was to find out the truth about Nixon's actions

    Ⓒ To highlight how Nixon managed to slow down congressional investigations

    Ⓓ To give a specific example of someone who resigned during the Saturday Night Massacre

Paragraph 4 is marked with an arrow [➡].

8. According to paragraph 5, Nixon was guilty of all of the following crimes EXCEPT

    Ⓐ misusing the powers granted to the leader

    Ⓑ attempting to disrupt a criminal investigation

    Ⓒ interfering in the vote count of a national election

    Ⓓ conspiring to hide evidence of criminal activity

Paragraph 5 is marked with an arrow [➡].

9. Look at the four squares [■] that indicate where the following sentence could be added to the passage.

    Ford believed that any criminal trials involving the former president would only cause further harm to American society.

    Where would the sentence best fit?

    Click on a square [■] to add the sentence to the passage.

10. **Directions:** An introductory sentence for a brief summary of the passage is provided below. Complete the summary by selecting the THREE answer choices that express the most important ideas in the passage. Some sentences do not belong in the summary because they express ideas that are not presented in the passage or are minor ideas in the passage. *This question is worth 2 points.*

    The Watergate break-in resulted in one of the worst political scandals in American history.
    -
    -
    -

Answer Choices

(A) President Nixon hired burglars to break into the headquarters of the Democratic Party to gather information that would help him in the 1972 election.

(B) The burglars were installing wiretaps and stealing documents when a security guard caught them and notified the police.

(C) Nixon lied to the American people about his involvement in the break-in and attempted to cover up evidence of the crime.

(D) Due to relentless congressional investigations, President Nixon was unable to pass any meaningful legislation during his second term in office.

(E) Nixon fought to end investigations into his administration but was forced to resign after recordings were released proving his guilt.

(F) American voters were outraged that a popular president was forced out of office and lost faith in their government.

    Drag your answer choices to the spaces where they belong. To remove an answer choice, click on it. To review the passage, click on **View Text**.

Organization

The Watergate Scandal

Introduction of the Watergate scandal

was a political scandal connected to U.S. President _____ _____'s reelection

Development of the scandal

• Political background of the time

┌ continued opposition to the _____ _____

└ was important for Nixon to win the 1972 reelection

• What Nixon's Committee and Presdient Nixon did

┌ hired _____ to break into the Democratic Party's office

├ tried to steal top-secret documents and _____ the phones

└ The president denied his involvement with the scandal and _____ the election.

Investigation of the scandal

┌ Former administration officials gave testimony.

├ Mass resignation, known as the _____ _____ _____, aroused public criticism.

└ The House of Representatives began formal _____ _____ against the president.

The truth uncovered

┌ The _____ _____ ordered the release of the recordings.

└ Nixon's attempt to conceal his involvement in the Watergate scandal was revealed.

The scandal's aftermath

┌ forced Nixon's resignation

└ caused great damage to American politics

Vocabulary Review

A **Fill in the blanks with the best answer. Change the form if necessary.**

aesthetic	reversal	burglar	legion	accumulation	aspiring

1. Hard training and encouragement are required for the success of _____ athletes.
2. The role _____ between the rich man and the poor man was humorously captured in the story.
3. Anyone who does not appreciate the _____ of this design does not understand architecture.
4. The efficiency of a military _____ depends on the obedience and discipline of the soldiers.
5. The prolific _____ has already served two years in jail after being caught on a security camera.

B **Choose the word that is closest in meaning to each highlighted word.**

1. The presidential candidate's touching address worked to his advantage.
   Ⓐ speech   Ⓑ change   Ⓒ location   Ⓓ scheme

2. A country's citizens are given certain privileges that non-citizens are not granted.
   Ⓐ advantages   Ⓑ tasks   Ⓒ limitations   Ⓓ problems

3. Water will generally dilute the concentration of nearly all solutions.
   Ⓐ increase   Ⓑ weaken   Ⓒ melt   Ⓓ complete

4. During the picnic, she discovered a long trail of ants that led to a small dirt mound.
   Ⓐ path   Ⓑ housing   Ⓒ hole   Ⓓ heap

5. The dictator's efforts to extend his term of office provoked a backlash.
   Ⓐ period   Ⓑ safety   Ⓒ popularity   Ⓓ finances

6. Many people work very hard to ascend the ranks of the corporate world.
   Ⓐ start   Ⓑ rise   Ⓒ finish   Ⓓ record

7. The survey results indicate that the general public approves of preventing the abuse of official authority.
   Ⓐ reinforcement   Ⓑ observation   Ⓒ exploitation   Ⓓ establishment

C **Choose the correct word in each sentence.**

1. During the (reign, resign) of Queen Elizabeth I, England enjoyed immense wealth.
2. Repairs were scheduled for the (malicious, malfunctioning) machines.
3. When the boys turn 21 years of age, they will (inherit, inhibit) the money that their grandmother left them.

Rhetorical Purpose

Vocabulary Preview

A   **Choose the word that best matches each definition.**

> Ⓐ observatory   Ⓑ conversely   Ⓒ convert
> Ⓓ ethical   Ⓔ drift   Ⓕ overboard

1. to change something in form: _____
2. over the side of a boat and into the water: _____
3. in an opposite or a very different way: _____
4. to move without any destination on water: _____
5. a building with equipment that enhances one's view of the sky: _____

B   **Choose the best synonym for each list of words.**

> Ⓐ comparatively   Ⓑ pollutant   Ⓒ adversely   Ⓓ sustained
> Ⓔ approximate   Ⓕ nuisance   Ⓖ recurring

1. bother   trouble   annoyance : _____
2. fairly   relatively   reasonably : _____
3. prolonged   lasting   continued : _____
4. repeated   habitual   continual : _____
5. guess   estimate   speculate : _____
6. disadvantageously   harmfully   negatively : _____

C   **Choose the right meaning for each highlighted word.**

1. One serious drawback to this exploration is the danger of wild animals.
   Ⓐ undesirable aspect   Ⓑ example that teaches a lesson

2. During basic training, a soldier learns how to withstand his own fears as well.
   Ⓐ to work in a team   Ⓑ to oppose something with determination

3. Certain types of fish can be easily found in a deep spot, about 150 meters offshore.
   Ⓐ straight down into water   Ⓑ in water and away from land

4. Economists project that stock prices of that internet-based company will plummet within the year.
   Ⓐ to dive suddenly and drastically   Ⓑ to endure and prove itself

5. Scientists extract natural substances from fruits, and medical companies produce vitamins with them.
   Ⓐ to measure with great accuracy   Ⓑ to withdraw or remove

Rhetorical Purpose

Introduction

- Rhetorical Purpose questions ask you why a piece of information has been presented in the passage in a certain way or particular place.

- 1 to 2 questions are given for each passage.

Question Types

Question forms that ask about the author's intent:

- Why does the author mention X in paragraph ___?
- Why does the author provide details about X in paragraph ___?
- The author discusses X in paragraph ___ in order to

Question forms that ask about the author's method:

- The author uses X as an example of
- How does the author explain the idea of X in paragraph ___?
- In paragraph ___, the author explains the concept of X by

Strategy

1. Infer the author's intention or his/her method of expression by locating the word/expression in the passage that is presented in the question and focusing on the logical connections between sentences and surrounding paragraphs.

2. Pre-learn expressions that often appear in answer choices.
   - **Explanation/Description:** to explain, to describe, to inform
   - **Definition:** to define, to identify
   - **Support/Refutation:** to support, to emphasize, to criticize, to argue
   - **Proof:** to prove, to show, to demonstrate, to give evidence that
   - **Comparison/Contrast:** to compare, to contrast
   - **Illustration:** to illustrate, to give/provide an example of

Basic Drills

The cotton gin was invented in 1793 by Eli Whitney. The machine, able to pull cotton fibers from cotton seeds, caused a revolution in cotton production in the Southern States. Before the cotton gin was invented, raising cotton was a very labor-intensive business, and separating the fiber from the seed itself required an even higher level of effort. However, this all changed as the cotton gin became more common, and, as a result, growing and cultivating cotton required less effort. Cotton became a lucrative cash crop, which in turn greatly helped cotton production in the South to rise. Consequently, the cotton gin revolutionized the cotton industry and made cotton one of the most important U.S. exports of the nineteenth century.

1 Why does the author mention the work environment before the invention of the cotton gin?

- Ⓐ To criticize the methods used by cotton workers
- Ⓑ To describe the hardship suffered by cotton workers
- Ⓒ To emphasize the important role the cotton gin played
- Ⓓ To give an example of alternative ways to produce cotton

Similar to other sciences, experimental psychology postulates that human behavior can be understood through detailed and well-controlled experiments carried out under laboratory conditions. Though widely practiced as a subfield of psychology, it has drawbacks. By closely controlling the surroundings of subjects, the researcher may create too artificial an environment. This means that although the researcher may have understood the "cause" of the subjects' behavior, the findings only apply under non-real world conditions and have limited use in explaining real-world behavior. Another weakness of the experimental method is that for ethical reasons, some questions cannot be studied using experiments. For example, it is important to note whether people who have had difficult rearing experiences, like living with poverty or abuse, continue to have problems in their adult years because of this poor rearing. However, we cannot place children in bad environments just to see if it causes damage that persists into adulthood.

2 Why does the author mention people who have had difficult rearing experiences?

- Ⓐ To show a specific case in which the experimental method cannot be used
- Ⓑ To identify subjects who are not suitable to be used in experiments
- Ⓒ To suggest that some people are easier to study than others
- Ⓓ To present an example of where experiments have been successfully carried out

Vocabulary

Choose the word that is closest in meaning to the underlined word in the passage.

1. lucrative	Ⓐ risky	Ⓑ profitable	Ⓒ popular	Ⓓ large-scale
2. postulates	Ⓐ theorizes	Ⓑ discards	Ⓒ disagrees	Ⓓ improves
3. persists	Ⓐ develops	Ⓑ fades	Ⓒ continues	Ⓓ changes

Reading Practice 01

Water that contains the dissolved minerals of calcium and magnesium is termed hard water to distinguish it from soft water, which usually refers to rainwater. Hard water is formed when water absorbs these minerals from rock and soil as it travels through the ground. Despite the presence of these minerals, hard water does not pose a health risk. Conversely, hard water can be a source of calcium and magnesium, both of which are necessary for good health.   5

Though it benefits health, hard water is a nuisance because it does not react well with various kinds of soap and its mineral content can damage pipes and appliances. When soaps and detergents mix with hard water, a sticky, abrasive curd-like substance is formed. Shampoo and soap do not lather well and therefore are not as effective. Skin loses its acidity and can become irritated, while hair can feel hard and appear lackluster. Clothes laundered in hard water come out 10 feeling rough and looking dull. Hard water is especially problematic on household surfaces and appliances. It causes a film to appear on shower walls, bathtubs, and sinks. Furthermore, when hard water is heated, the minerals separate out of the water and the result is scaling – when the precipitation of minerals forms a limestone deposit. This buildup causes clogging in drainpipes and in appliances such as coffee makers and kettles.   15

The most common and economically viable way to soften water is by using a water softener. This device puts the water through a process of ion replacement. As the hard water flows through a bed of sodium-charged beads, the calcium and magnesium ions trade places with the sodium ions, which do not create scale or react badly with soap.

Glossary

sodium: a common soft, silver-white metallic element of the alkali group that is found in salt

1   The author mentions rainwater in order to

    Ⓐ provide an example of soft water

    Ⓑ present similarities between hard and soft water

    Ⓒ provide information about the source of calcium in hard water

    Ⓓ show how soft water is transformed to hard water

2   Why does the author mention coffee makers and kettles?

    Ⓐ To provide an example of the things hard water causes problems for

    Ⓑ To explain how to get rid of scaling in home appliances

    Ⓒ To present problems caused by clogging in appliances

    Ⓓ To discuss some appliances that do not suffer from scaling

3   Why does the author mention ion replacement?

    Ⓐ To provide an example of how mineral separation can be reversed

    Ⓑ To suggest an alternative use for hard water

    Ⓒ To explain how to soften hard water

    Ⓓ To identify the most frequent cause of water hardening

Summary

Unlike soft water, hard water contains the dissolved _____ of calcium and magnesium which cause many problems. Although it has _____ benefits for humans, hard water does not react well with soap and can negatively affect washed hair and clothes, making them appear dull. It causes a(n) _____ to appear on household surfaces, while pipes and appliances experience scale, a buildup of limestone deposits left by the minerals in the water. A(n) _____ _____ can be used to soften the water through a process of _____ _____.

Reading Practice 02

The bottle gourd is an annual herb that is a member of the same family as squashes and melons. It is indigenous to Africa and is believed to be one of the first plants cultivated by humans, thousands of years ago. Although it was occasionally used as a source of food or medicine, the bottle gourd was most valued for its hard-shelled dried fruit. Multi-functional bottle gourds were used by ancient people all around the world as floats for nets, containers for water, 5 eating utensils, and even as musical instruments. What botanists are unsure of, however, is exactly how the bottle gourd was initially transported from Africa to Asia and the New World.

The prevailing theory is that bottle gourds simply drifted across the ocean, perhaps as an indirect result of African farmers transporting their crops by river. Bottle gourds are extremely buoyant, so if any were to fall overboard during these trips, they were likely to be carried by 10 the river's currents to the open sea, where they would be swept away by ocean tides. Modern researchers have proven that the bottle gourd is able to withstand such a journey, capable of floating in the ocean for hundreds of days and still possessing seeds from which new gourds can be grown.

There are others who believe that the bottle gourd was brought to the New World by ocean- 15 faring African fishermen. The basis of this argument is that any naturally dispersed bottle gourds would have been washed up on New World beaches, an environment in which they do not naturally grow and thus could not survive in. Therefore, humans had to have played a part in their appearance in the New World. Most botanists, however, refute this theory. They claim those bottle gourds that floated across the ocean may have been carried inland by strong waves or hurricanes 20 to more suitable ecological sites. Subsequently, they claim, the native tribes of the New World may have domesticated them.

1   Why does the author mention hard-shelled dried fruit?

(A) To provide evidence that bottle gourds were cultivated

(B) To identify the various functions of bottle gourds

(C) To show how bottle gourds were used as medicine

(D) To explain why bottle gourds received so much attention from scientists

2   The author mentions the buoyancy of bottle gourds in order to

(A) explain why African fishermen transported them by river

(B) imply that humans were required to move them in strong currents

(C) describe a feature of gourds that could make natural dispersion possible

(D) identify one of the most important features of the bottle gourds

3   The author explains the dispersion of the bottle gourd by

(A) contrasting arguments put forward for natural and human dispersion

(B) identifying the most common reason for their dispersion

(C) listing evidence that supports natural and human dispersion

(D) explaining how marine life played a part in the process

Organization

- Bottle gourds — had various functions: food, medicine, floats for nets, containers for _____, etc.
- Two theories about how bottle gourds reached Asia and the _____ _____
  - natural dispersion ─┬─ drifted across the _____
                        └─ capable of floating on the ocean for hundreds of days
  - human dispersion ─┬─ brought by _____ _____
                      └─ cannot grow on beaches, thus humans played a part in their dispersion

iBT Practice 01

Edwin Hubble

Edwin Powell Hubble, astronomer and founder of modern cosmology, was born in Missouri in 1889. He earned a degree in mathematics and astronomy at the University of Chicago in 1910 and went on to become a Rhodes scholar at Oxford University in England, receiving a degree in law. However, he soon became bored with the practice of law and chose instead to return to his investigations of astronomy. Mt. Wilson Observatory in California, home of the largest and most technologically advanced telescope in the world, became his base of research in 1919.   5

→ Hubble's first major discovery in the field of astronomy came in 1923. At that time, scientists were still uncertain whether our galaxy, the Milky Way, constituted the universe in its entirety, or was instead simply one of many such star clusters contained within a much larger space. While observing the Andromeda nebula, he found that it contained a Cepheid – a *variable star* that regularly changes in terms of brightness. Using the recent work of another American   10 astronomer who had determined how to calculate the distance to a Cepheid, Hubble was able to approximate its distance from Earth. He found that this Cepheid was so far away that it could not be inside our galaxy, but outside the Milky Way, as was the Andromeda nebula. Thus, he realized that the Andromeda nebula itself was a separate galaxy, proving definitively the vast size of our universe.   15

→ In 1929, Hubble made a second revolutionary discovery, this one based on a study of light spectra received from other galaxies. The light spectra emitted by a galaxy increase in wavelength when observed from Earth. This shift to longer wavelengths is a phenomenon that occurs when a galaxy is moving away from Earth. After examining the light spectra of many galaxies, Hubble found that all of them followed this pattern of wavelength shifts, and the farther   20 away the galaxy, the greater the shift. This discovery allowed Hubble to propose that galaxies were moving away from Earth at a rate proportional to their distance from our planet – that is, the farther away a galaxy is from Earth, the faster that galaxy is moving away from Earth. This observation became known as Hubble's law and provided the first evidence that the universe expands over time.   25

→ Hubble's realization about the wavelength shifts led him to take a further step. He reasoned that if galaxies are traveling away from each other at a speed proportionate to their distance, they must have started their cosmic expansion from the same space at the same time. In other words, Hubble's observation that this expansion is approximately uniform provided confirmation for the Big Bang theory, which says the universe came into existence with an   30 immense burst of energy and has been expanding ever since. He calculated that this explosion must have occurred about two billion years ago. Although more recent estimates have dated the Big Bang to approximately 20 billion years ago, this should not take away from the fact that Hubble's discoveries permanently changed the way people view the universe.

1. The word constituted in the passage is closest in meaning to
    (A) permitted   (B) made up   (C) designed   (D) went through

2. The word it in the passage refers to
    (A) Milky Way   (B) Andromeda nebula
    (C) Earth   (D) Cepheid

3. According to paragraph 2, how did Hubble calculate the distance to a Cepheid in the Andromeda nebula?
    (A) By drawing on the research of one of his contemporaries
    (B) By hypothesizing that the Andromeda nebula was outside the Milky Way
    (C) By questioning and revising the work of his peers in the scientific community
    (D) By studying the movement of variable stars
    Paragraph 2 is marked with an arrow [→].

4. All of the following are mentioned in paragraph 3 as part of Hubble's law EXCEPT
    (A) all galaxies emit light that possesses a similar wavelength
    (B) our universe continually grows larger as time goes by
    (C) the speed of a galaxy's movement is related to its distance from Earth
    (D) light recorded from other galaxies increases in wavelength
    Paragraph 3 is marked with an arrow [→].

5. The word immense in the passage is closest in meaning to
    (A) enormous   (B) explosive   (C) fierce   (D) unexpected

6. Why does the author mention that the Big Bang may have occurred about 20 billion years ago in paragraph 4?
    (A) To describe Hubble's most remarkable achievement
    (B) To admit that scientists still do not know the universe's age
    (C) To note that Hubble did not accurately date the Big Bang
    (D) To express doubt about the Big Bang theory
    Paragraph 4 is marked with an arrow [→].

7. **Directions:** An introductory sentence for a brief summary of the passage is provided below. Complete the summary by selecting the THREE answer choices that express the most important ideas in the passage. Some sentences do not belong in the summary because they express ideas that are not presented in the passage or are minor ideas in the passage. ***This question is worth 2 points.***

> The American astronomer Edwin Powell Hubble made some of the most important discoveries about our universe.
>
> •
>
> •
>
> •

Answer Choices

(A) Though Hubble proposed a theory on the origins of the universe, he failed to calculate the exact age of the universe.

(B) Hubble began a scientific debate over whether our Milky Way galaxy filled the entire universe.

(C) By studying a variable star in the Andromeda nebula, Hubble was able to show that the universe is composed of multiple galaxies.

(D) It was a careful study of the wavelengths of light spectra from distant galaxies that led Hubble to one of his most important findings.

(E) One of his major discoveries, now known as Hubble's law, holds that galaxies are traveling away from Earth.

(F) His proposal about the expansion of the universe upheld the Big Bang theory and helped establish Hubble as a significant twentieth-century astronomer.

> Drag your answer choices to the spaces where they belong. To remove an answer choice, click on it. To review the passage, click on **View Text**.

● iBT Practice 02

The Dust Bowl

The "Dust Bowl" refers to an area of the Great Plains in the United States comprised of parts of Colorado, Kansas, Oklahoma, and Texas, much of which was severely hit by dust storms in the 1930s. The disaster, which lasted about a decade, resulted in turning the once fertile farmland in the region into a desert of around 100 million acres, causing hundreds of thousands of people to flee their homes.

The causes of the Dust Bowl disaster can be traced to a combination of factors; most notably poor management of land due to wheat production and periods of sustained drought. Prior to the 1930s, the Great Plains were covered with grass, which served to hold the soil in place. Problems began, however, when farmers were encouraged to grow increasing amounts of wheat in order to meet the rising demand for this grain. To meet this demand, they turned vital grassland into fields for wheat cultivation. They plowed more and more fields, increasing their production to meet the demand, and when the price of wheat plummeted due to oversupply, the farmers did not relent in their wheat farming, hoping to make the same profit regardless of soil conservation practices. To exacerbate the situation, extreme droughts occurred about every two years during the 1930s which increased in severity, making it impossible for the land to recover.

From 1934 onward, severe dust storms, or black blizzards, occurred as the land dried up. ■ Extreme winds blew the dry, loose soil into large clouds of dust and sand that covered an area of 10,000 feet. ■ They were so thick and big that they obscured the sun, sometimes for days at a time. ■ It was not uncommon for these blizzards to blow off 3 to 4 inches of precious topsoil. ■

The dire conditions of the Great Plains brought about an economic crisis which caused a mass migration of farming families west into neighboring states. Hundreds of thousands, if not millions, of people were displaced, causing the largest migration in American history. The migrants, the majority of whom were from Oklahoma, moved to California, Oregon, or Washington.

➔ It was not until 1935 that serious efforts were made by local and state governments to find a solution to the crisis by developing ways of soil conservation and erosion-prevention farming methods. The planting of grass, crop rotation, less aggressive plowing, and the planting of trees as a shelter belt were put into practice. These measures significantly reduced the amount of topsoil that was blown away, and when the 1940s came, the periods of extreme drought had subsided.

1. The word they in the passage refers to

    (A) Great Plains   (B) problems   (C) farmers   (D) amounts of wheat

2. Which of the sentences below best expresses the essential information in the highlighted sentence in the passage? *Incorrect* choices change the meaning in important ways or leave out essential information.

    (A) More and more farmers plowed fields and grew wheat in order to make profits from the increased demand for wheat.

    (B) Because traditional soil conservation practices were not providing enough profit, farmers turned to wheat production to earn more money.

    (C) Though wheat prices went down because of a decline in demand, farmers kept growing more wheat.

    (D) The farmers kept growing more wheat to try to maintain profit levels in the face of oversupply despite the damage it was doing to the soil.

3. The word exacerbate in the passage is closest in meaning to

    (A) end   (B) worsen   (C) improve   (D) change

4. Why does the author mention the largest migration in American history?

    (A) To identify the reason for the economic disaster in the Dust Bowl

    (B) To provide an explanation for population increases in the Great Plains during the 1930s

    (C) To introduce other Dust Bowl cities that suffered

    (D) To illustrate the enormous impact of the Dust Bowl disaster

5. All of the following are mentioned in paragraph 5 as measures local and state governments took EXCEPT

    (A) using improved plows

    (B) creating a wind barrier

    (C) employing crop rotation

    (D) planting grass

    Paragraph 5 is marked with an arrow [➡].

6. Look at the four squares [■] that indicate where the following sentence could be added to the passage.

> Because of this effect, dust storms took the name black blizzards.

Where would the sentence best fit?

> Click on a square [■] to add the sentence to the passage.

7. **Directions:** An introductory sentence for a brief summary of the passage is provided below. Complete the summary by selecting the THREE answer choices that express the most important ideas in the passage. Some sentences do not belong in the summary because they express ideas that are not presented in the passage or are minor ideas in the passage. ***This question is worth 2 points.***

> In the 1930s, environmental disaster struck the Great Plains in the United States.
>
> -
> -
> -

Answer Choices

- Ⓐ In the Great Plains, a great amount of topsoil was blown off by severe dust storms.
- Ⓑ Poor land management and recurring droughts meant that the crops being produced by farmers caused irreversible damage to the land.
- Ⓒ By 1935, measures were being taken by government authorities to solve the problems caused by the dust storms.
- Ⓓ Massive storms of dust swept through the Great Plains, destroying land and leaving people with no choice other than to leave the region.
- Ⓔ By concentrating on wheat production to meet high demand, farmers were able to earn more profits than before.
- Ⓕ With the decrease in dust storms in the 1940s, fields which had been destroyed earlier fully recovered.

> Drag your answer choices to the spaces where they belong. To remove an answer choice, click on it. To review the passage, click on **View Text**.

Actual **Practice Test**

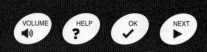

The Energy of the Oceans

Renewable energy from the oceans comes in various forms – thermal difference, tides, and waves – and can amount to enormous sums of energy. In order to derive electrical power from these high energy densities, methods of generation are being investigated worldwide.

Being the earth's largest solar collectors, oceans are able to generate huge amounts of thermal energy from the sun. Solar heat warms the surface water to a much greater extent than ⁵ the deep ocean water, and this difference can be used to generate electricity. A process called Ocean Thermal Energy Conversion (OTEC) utilizes the heat energy in the earth's oceans to produce electricity.

➡ OTEC systems can be either of two types depending on the thermodynamic cycle – closed-cycle or open-cycle. Closed-cycle OTEC utilizes liquid with a low boiling point, like ¹⁰ propane or ammonia, as an intermediate fluid. The first step is for the OTEC plant to pump in warm seawater and boil the intermediate fluid. After that, the intermediate fluid vapor moves the turbine to generate electricity. Finally, cold seawater cools the vapor. Open-cycle OTEC is only different in that it does not use an intermediate fluid. The warm seawater on the ocean surface pushes the turbine after being turned into low-pressure vapor. ¹⁵

■ Although there are now several experimental OTEC plants, none of them are large operations. ■ That is because OTEC power plants require huge initial investments, and there are not many land-based sites where deep-ocean water is close enough to shore to make OTEC plants practical. ■ However, it is comparatively clean and will not add to global warming through the production of pollutants. ■ ²⁰

➡ Tidal power uses the power created by changes in the level of the oceans caused by the gravitational effect of the moon and the sun, and the rotation of the earth. Because water levels can vary by up to 40 feet close to shore, the tidal range is sufficiently large to produce energy economically. A type of dam called a barrage is normally used to convert tidal energy into electricity. Gates and turbines allow the water to pass through the dam. When the tide has ²⁵ stopped coming in, the gates are closed, trapping the water within the basin or estuary; as the tide recedes, the gates are opened. As the water flows through these gates, the turbines are driven, thus generating power.

Tidal power plants do not cost a lot to operate, but their construction costs are high and payback periods are lengthy. In addition, since a tidal barrage can change the tidal level in a ³⁰ basin, it may cause flooding of the shoreline, which can adversely affect both the local marine food chain and sea life migration.

➡ Wave power is another method to harness the ocean's energy by extracting energy directly from surface waves or from pressure changes below the surface. Both offshore and

onshore systems can transform wave energy into electricity. Offshore systems are situated in 35
deep water and use the bobbing motion of the waves. The rise and fall of the waves pressurizes
the water, and the pressure fluctuations rotate a turbine, creating electricity. Onshore systems
concentrate the waves into a narrow channel that feeds into a reservoir built on cliffs above
sea level. Waves increase in height as the channel narrows, and the water that flows out of this
reservoir spins turbines that generate electricity. 40

Nowadays, because of their inability to compete with traditional energy sources and higher
costs, there are not any big commercial wave energy plants – just a few small companies. On a
positive note, however, wave energy plants have a long-term operational lifetime; also, because
onshore wave energy systems can be incorporated into harbor walls, they can serve as a barrier,
protecting buildings by the shore. 45

1. According to paragraph 3, the classification of systems as "closed-cycle OTEC" or "open-cycle
   OTEC" is determined by
   (A) the boiling point of the intermediate liquid
   (B) the inclusion of a turbine
   (C) the pumping of seawater
   (D) the use of an intermediate fluid
   Paragraph 3 is marked with an arrow [➤].

2. Which of the following is a reason why OTEC plants are not large operations?
   (A) Because they have an operational lifetime that is too short
   (B) Because there is a lack of technology to make them productive
   (C) Because they require too many start-up costs
   (D) Because they cannot be competitive with traditional power companies

3. According to paragraph 5, which of the following is NOT true of tidal power?
   (A) It utilizes a kind of dam to generate electricity.
   (B) It uses power created by changes in sea levels.
   (C) It is capable of producing electricity economically.
   (D) It generates power from the incoming tide.
   Paragraph 5 is marked with an arrow [➤].

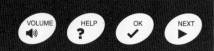

4. Which of the sentences below best expresses the essential information in the highlighted sentence in the passage? *Incorrect* choices change the meaning in important ways or leave out essential information.

    Ⓐ Marine life can be negatively impacted by shoreline flooding caused by changes in tidal levels resulting from the use of a tidal barrage.

    Ⓑ Tidal barrages can be adversely affected by shoreline flooding, which in turn can cause problems for the marine food chain.

    Ⓒ To prevent flooding of the shoreline, tidal barrages are used to change tidal levels in a basin.

    Ⓓ The use of tidal barrages promotes sea life migration by changing the tidal level.

5. The word fluctuations in the passage is closest in meaning to

    Ⓐ swings   Ⓑ increases

    Ⓒ standards   Ⓓ supplies

6. According to paragraph 7, which of the following is true of the onshore system?

    Ⓐ It uses reservoirs constructed above sea level to generate electricity.

    Ⓑ It employs wide channels to feed water into electrical turbines.

    Ⓒ It utilizes the motion of waves to power electricity-generating turbines.

    Ⓓ It generates substantially more power than offshore systems can.

    Paragraph 7 is marked with an arrow [➡].

7. The word their in the passage refers to

    Ⓐ waves   Ⓑ turbines

    Ⓒ wave energy plants   Ⓓ small companies

8. The author mentions a barrier in order to

    Ⓐ provide an example of a benefit of an onshore wave energy system

    Ⓑ explain how harbor walls can be protected from danger

    Ⓒ show why wave energy plants cost more to operate

    Ⓓ suggest an alternative use for wave energy plants

9. Look at the four squares [■] that indicate where the following sentence could be added to the passage.

> In addition, as ocean thermal energy is a reasonably constant source, OTEC technology has a lot of potential to develop.

Where would the sentence best fit?

Click on a square [■] to add the sentence to the passage.

10. **Directions:** Complete the table by matching the phrases below. Select the appropriate phrases from the answer choices and match them to the type of ocean energy to which they relate. TWO of the answer choices will NOT be used. *This question is worth 4 points.*

Drag your answer choices to the spaces where they belong. To remove an answer choice, click on it. To review the passage, click on **View Text**.

Answer Choices		Thermal energy
Ⓐ Uses a barrage in the conversion process to produce electricity	▶	
Ⓑ Provides both energy and pure water at the same time	▶	
Ⓒ Is made possible by differences in surface and deep water temperatures	▶	
Ⓓ Uses onshore and offshore systems		Tidal energy
Ⓔ Is one of the causes of global warming	▶	
Ⓕ Is unable to compete with traditional energy sources	▶	
Ⓖ Suffers from a lack of suitable sites that can generate electricity		Wave energy
Ⓗ Uses warm seawater in the production of energy	▶	
Ⓘ Generates electricity at a low cost	▶	

Organization

The Energy of the Oceans

Introduction

　　Renewable energy from the ocean: _____ difference, tides, and _____

Three types of ocean energy

① Thermal energy

    ┌ Closed-cycle OTEC: warm seawater is used to bring a(n) _____ _____ to
    │   a boil / the intermediate fluid vapor causes a turbine to generate
    │   electricity
    └ Open-cycle OTEC: warm seawater is converted to _____, causing a turbine to
                   generate electricity

    ┌ Weakness: expensive start-up costs / lack of an appropriate _____ for OTEC plants
    └ Strength: a relatively clean source of energy

② Tidal energy

    _____ (barrage): traps and releases tidal flows to spin turbines

    ┌ Strength: low operating costs
    └ Weakness: high _____ costs / has a damaging effect on the coastal environment

③ Wave energy

    ┌ Offshore systems: situated in deep water / _____ changes power turbines
    └ Onshore systems: built on cliffs above _____ _____ / waves move through
                   channels to _____ turbines

    ┌ Weakness: not competitive with _____ energy sources
    └ Strength: can remain operational for long periods of time / can protect the shore
                   environment

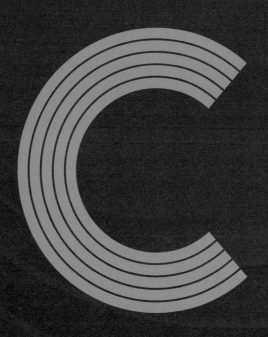

PART

C

Recognizing Organization

Insertion

Vocabulary Preview

A **Choose the word that best matches each definition.**

Ⓐ myriad	Ⓑ stance	Ⓒ bloom
Ⓓ host	Ⓔ inherent	Ⓕ coiled

1. to open, as in a flower: _____
2. mental attitude toward something: _____
3. arranged in a series of loops: _____
4. existing as an essential part of something: _____
5. a living organism inside which another living organism can be entirely supported: _____

B **Choose the best synonym for each list of words.**

Ⓐ dimension	Ⓑ archetype	Ⓒ squirt	Ⓓ catastrophe
Ⓔ eruption	Ⓕ class	Ⓖ transparent	

1. tragedy   misfortune   disaster   : _____
2. measurement   size   extent   : _____
3. original   prototype   standard   : _____
4. see-through   clear   crystalline : _____
5. spurt   shoot   burst   : _____
6. kind   sort   category   : _____

C **Choose the right meaning for each highlighted word or phrase.**

1. The exchange of commodities before the invention of money is called barter.
   - Ⓐ skills and knowledge
   - Ⓑ things of some value

2. The scholarship foundation at the university was formed to spur scientific research.
   - Ⓐ to scout people with potential
   - Ⓑ to encourage something

3. After the hurricane, the harbor was a scene of disaster, with drifting fish boats heading every direction.
   - Ⓐ moving in a constant direction
   - Ⓑ moving slowly carried by external forces

4. Much to our surprise, a certain type of tree that was thought to have been extinct has reappeared in the area.
   - Ⓐ suited to a different location
   - Ⓑ completely disappeared and ceased to exist

5. Chang Rae Lee's *Native Speaker* is likened to Ellison's *Invisible Man* by these particular scholars.
   - Ⓐ compared with
   - Ⓑ analyzed as

Insertion

Introduction

- Insertion questions focus on your understanding of the flow of the passage and the logical connection between its sentences.

- A new sentence is provided, and you must select and click on one of the four squares [■] to indicate where the new sentence best fits.

- 0 to 1 questions are given for each passage.

Question Type

Look at the four squares [■] that indicate where the following sentence could be added to the passage.

[A sentence in bold will appear here.]

Where would the sentence best fit?

Click on a square [■] to add the sentence to the passage.

Strategy

1. Carefully note the flow of the passage and words that provide clues to the logical link between sentences. Also, pay close attention to the new sentence and those sentences around each square [■]. Clue words that are often used are as follows:

   1) Indicative words

      The object that the indicative word refers to is usually located in the sentence before the one that has the indicative word.

   2) Transition words

      Transition words make the flow of the passage natural and they help establish clear connections between sentences.

   3) Same word/Synonym

      Sometimes, two sentences placed close together share a word/phrase, or a word/phrase is used in one sentence and a synonym/synonymous phrase is used in the other.

2. Insert the new sentence at the selected square [■] and make sure it flows naturally with the surrounding sentences.

Basic Drills

Marina City, towering above the banks of the Chicago River on North State Street, is a complex consisting of two cylindrical towers with balconies designed to look like petals. ■ Because of their <u>distinctive</u> shape, the towers have been given the nickname of the "corn cobs." ■ Upon its completion in 1964, Marina City was the largest concrete building in the world, and its design differed from the then architectural <u>practice</u> of straight lines and cubical apartments. ■ The thinking behind the cylindrical shape was to decrease wind pressure, while concrete was used because it is the only material suitable to construct petal-shaped apartments. ■ It is one of Chicago's best known landmarks and <u>reinforced</u> the city's reputation as a leader of modern urban architecture.

1　Look at the four squares [■] that indicate where the following sentence could be added to the passage.

> These "corn-cob" towers were designed in 1959 by Bertrand Goldberg and took five years to construct.

Where would the sentence best fit?

Located in the rain forests of Indonesia, rafflesia flowers are the largest single flowers on Earth. The rafflesia is a rare flower made up of five leathery petals that can grow to over 90 centimeters in diameter. ■ Furthermore, it lives almost entirely within its host, a group of vines, by spreading its thread-like strands completely within their cells. ■ The leaves, roots, and stem of the rafflesia cannot be seen until the reproduction stage, at which time flowers bud through the woody vine and blossom into the amazing spectacle for which they are world-famous. ■ It can take as much as ten months for the flowers to develop from the initial visible bud to the state of blooming. ■ Upon blooming, the rafflesia gives off a <u>repulsive</u> odor like rotting meat, which attracts insects that pollinate the plant.

2　Look at the four squares [■] that indicate where the following sentence could be added to the passage.

> Compared to the long period of preparation for blooming, the spectacular bloom may last no more than a few days.

Where would the sentence best fit?

Vocabulary

Choose the word that is closest in meaning to the underlined word in the passage.

1. distinctive　　Ⓐ amazing　　Ⓑ superior　　Ⓒ horrible　　Ⓓ unique
2. practice　　　　Ⓐ custom　　　Ⓑ improvement　Ⓒ shape　　　Ⓓ standard
3. reinforced　　　Ⓐ removed　　Ⓑ approved　　Ⓒ strengthened　Ⓓ created
4. repulsive　　　 Ⓐ disgusting　Ⓑ powerful　　Ⓒ flowery　　Ⓓ unusual

Cephalopods are a class of <u>mollusks</u> including nautiluses, octopuses, squids, and cuttlefish. They live in a wide range of ocean habitats and even, in a few cases, in fresh water. They vary widely in size and lifestyle. Their origins date back to the Late Cambrian period, almost 500 million years ago.

Features that cephalopods have in common include numerous arms with suckers; three [5] hearts; blue blood; a stiff, curved beak; large brains; and, in most cases, sophisticated eyes. Nautiluses are the most primitive cephalopods. They have coiled shells and a myriad of arms – more than ninety. Octopuses have no shells, rounded bodies, and eight arms. Squids and cuttlefish look similar, with bullet-shaped bodies, eight arms, and two tentacles each. Cuttlefish can be distinguished by their broader internal shells compared to squids and their w-shaped [10] pupils.

Cephalopods can be found in every part of the ocean. Octopuses and nautiluses live deep in the ocean, while squids and cuttlefish live in the open ocean and often move between deep and shallow layers frequently. ■ There are two main ways cephalopods move: by flapping their arms and fins or by jet propulsion, filling their mantles with water and forcing it out of their tentacle [15] ends at high speeds. ■ That is not the most impressive thing about these creatures, though. ■ Compared to other invertebrates, cephalopods are highly intelligent and have displayed well-developed memories and problem-solving abilities. ■ As a group, octopuses, squids, and cuttlefish display an array of remarkable abilities, from squirting ink to changing colors to bioluminescence. [20]

■ Cephalopod species meet in large numbers to spawn. ■ Males will transfer bundles of sperm into the mantles of females who then lay clusters of egg capsules. ■ Cephalopods are not long-lived and most species die after reproducing. ■ The eggs hatch after some months and the next generation swims away, some feeding on drifting food particles and some already able to hunt.

Glossary

mollusk: a type of sea or land animal that has a soft body covered by a hard shell

1 Look at the four squares [■] in paragraph 3 that indicate where the following sentence could be added to the passage.

Squids, for example, generate jets that can move them up to eight meters a second.

Where would the sentence best fit?

Click on a square [■] to add the sentence to the passage.

2 Look at the four squares [■] in paragraph 4 that indicate where the following sentence could be added to the passage.

These abilities are often used for defense and hunting, but also communication, especially during courtship.

Where would the sentence best fit?

Click on a square [■] to add the sentence to the passage.

Extra Question

According to paragraph 2, which of the following is true about features of cephalopods?

(A) They have suckers on their arms.

(B) Many of them have bad eyesight.

(C) They have eight to nine arms.

(D) None of them have shells.

Summary

Cephalopods are _____-dwelling mollusks with ancient origins and a striking variety of sizes, lifestyles, and abilities. They include the primitive, large-shelled nautiluses; round- and soft-bodied _____; and bullet-bodied _____ and cuttlefish. These creatures have highly developed brains and eyes, and also surprising defensive and communication mechanisms, such as squirting _____ and changing color. Their life cycles are typically only a couple of years; they die after they lay their eggs, leaving their hatchlings to grow up without them.

Reading Practice 02

The eye is an extremely complex organ, spherical in shape and often likened to a camera for the way in which it focuses and processes light from external objects. ■ In fact, it is because of light that we can see shapes, colors, brightness, distance, and dimensions of objects. ■ In the absence of light, the eye cannot see. ■ Although the process of vision begins with the eye, the process of seeing is performed by the brain. ■

5

The process of vision begins when light waves bounce off the surface of objects and travel into the eye through the cornea, the transparent dome-shaped covering at the front of the eye. As it passes through the cornea, light is refracted and transformed into electrical signals. The light then moves through the pupil, the black circular opening in the middle of the eye that is controlled by surrounding muscle which, depending on the amount of light, can constrict or dilate. The light is further refracted by the lens which is situated directly behind the black pupil and colored (e.g., brown, blue, or green) <u>iris</u>. ■ The lens is composed of many tiny fibers and works together with the cornea to project an inverted image onto the multi-layered retina, which is a large layer of nerve tissue that lines the back of the eye. ■ Light impulses on the retina are changed into millions of electrical signals and then sent through the optic nerve, along the visual pathway, to the visual area of the brain. ■ Here brain cells translate the electrical signals into a visual image, providing us with sight. ■ Because light rays are focused in the retina upside down, the signals are rearranged when the brain processes them into an image that is the right way up.

10

15

1 Look at the four squares [■] in paragraph 1 that indicate where the following sentence could be added to the passage.

These two organs work together to produce vision.

Where would the sentence best fit?

Click on a square [■] to add the sentence to the passage.

2 Look at the four squares [■] in paragraph 2 that indicate where the following sentence could be added to the passage.

If the eye is considered to be a type of camera, the retina is the film.

Where would the sentence best fit?

Click on a square [■] to add the sentence to the passage.

Extra Question

According to the passage, human eyes control the amount of light by

(A) making the fibers of the lens dilate

(B) focusing light rays in the multi-layered retina

(C) refracting light through the cornea

(D) enlarging or constricting the muscle around the pupil

Summary

While the process of vision begins with the eye, it is the _____ that "sees." Light waves travel into the eye through the _____. The light is refracted and transformed into electrical signals before it passes through the pupil. The _____, which sits behind the pupil, further refracts the light. With the cornea, the lens projects a(n) _____ image onto the _____. Light impulses on the retina are changed into millions of electrical signals and then sent through the _____ _____ to the visual area of the brain. The brain cells translate the signals into a visual image, providing us with _____.

● iBT Practice 01

The Architecture of Frank Lloyd Wright

Considered by most experts to be the greatest architect of the twentieth century, Frank Lloyd Wright was a true original whose buildings and ideas represent some of the most significant architectural works of modern times. Wright thought of his style of architecture as "organic," focusing on order, structure, and form in relation to nature. Wright subscribed to the power of good design to help people become aware and respectful of their surroundings and nature. In 70 years of creating revolutionary architecture, Wright designed over 1,000 works, from houses and offices to churches and museums. Of his total designs, 532 were constructed and 409 remain standing today.

→ A large number of Wright's most well-known buildings are houses. Wright wanted to design a new type of home in the middle-class suburban neighborhoods of Chicago and consequently built "prairie houses" between 1900 and 1917. Named after the vast flat areas of land between the Mississippi River and the Rocky Mountains, prairie houses reflected the atmosphere of the Chicago suburbs where they were built. Most of the time, these long, horizontal, and mostly one-story structures consisted of wide-open spaces instead of strictly defined rooms. Furthermore, they intentionally blurred the distinction between indoor space and the surrounding landscape.

Wright's insistence on blending his architecture into its natural surroundings reached its peak in 1935 with his creation of the magnificent house "Fallingwater" in Mill Run, Pennsylvania. Rated as the finest private house of the twentieth century, it is a perfect example of Wright's vision of harmony between man and nature. Wright located the house over a running stream and waterfall while anchoring it in the rock next to the falls. The house's outdoor ledges boast terraces that look down on the stream and the rest of the natural landscape surrounding the home.

→ Perhaps the most famous of Wright's creations is the Guggenheim Museum in New York, which opened shortly after his death in 1959. ■ The Guggenheim Museum is a classic example of his efforts to represent the inherent flexibility of organic forms in architecture. ■ The Guggenheim's external architecture appears like a spiral-shaped white snail or shell reaching upward above the street. ■ Its inside is also similar to that of a seashell, and its unique geometry allows visitors to easily experience the artwork on display. ■ This is done by taking an elevator to the top level and then viewing the individual paintings by walking down the gradually descending spiral ramp in the structure's center. Divided like the membranes in citrus fruit, the galleries include self-contained yet interdependent sections.

1. The word blurred in the passage is closest in meaning to
   - (A) harmed
   - (B) removed
   - (C) emphasized
   - (D) obscured

2. According to paragraph 2, which of the following is NOT true about "prairie houses"?
   - (A) They imitated the nature of the Chicago suburbs.
   - (B) They usually contained open floor plans.
   - (C) They were typically long and horizontal.
   - (D) They were the most common home design in Chicago.

   Paragraph 2 is marked with an arrow [➡].

3. The word anchoring in the passage is closest in meaning to
   - (A) retaining
   - (B) securing
   - (C) modeling
   - (D) catching

4. Why does the author mention the membranes in citrus fruit?
   - (A) To imply that the Guggenheim Museum had a complicated design structure
   - (B) To show where Wright got the design idea for the Guggenheim Museum
   - (C) To suggest the nature of the artwork being displayed in the Guggenheim Museum
   - (D) To describe how Wright incorporated organic forms in the Guggenheim Museum

5. According to paragraph 4, what is the purpose of the Guggenheim's geometry?
   - (A) It facilitates the viewing of the art exhibits.
   - (B) It reduces visitors' movement to a minimum.
   - (C) It reflects the surrounding environment.
   - (D) It allows for more artwork to be displayed.

   Paragraph 4 is marked with an arrow [➡].

6. Look at the four squares [■] that indicate where the following sentence could be added to the passage.

    > Its spiral design is very different from the more traditional angular structures common to New York City.

    Where would the sentence best fit?

    > Click on a square [■] to add the sentence to the passage.

7. **Directions:** An introductory sentence for a brief summary of the passage is provided below. Complete the summary by selecting the THREE answer choices that express the most important ideas in the passage. Some sentences do not belong in the summary because they express ideas that are not presented in the passage or are minor ideas in the passage. ***This question is worth 2 points.***

    > With an organic style and a focus on the relationship between design and nature, Frank Lloyd Wright became the twentieth-century's greatest architect.
    >
    > -
    > -
    > -

    Answer Choices

    (A) The "Fallingwater" house stands as the pinnacle of Wright's notion that homes should reflect their natural surroundings.

    (B) Taking their name from the type of land found in the central U.S., the "prairie houses" of Chicago were revolutionary.

    (C) Almost all of the structures that Wright designed, from office buildings to churches, are still in use today.

    (D) In the early 1900s, Wright's prairie houses redefined the nature of homes in the middle-class Chicago suburbs.

    (E) Wright's work on the Guggenheim Museum best represents his organic style and is his most famous design.

    (F) Wright included a descending spiral ramp in the design of the Guggenheim Museum.

    > Drag your answer choices to the spaces where they belong. To remove an answer choice, click on it. To review the passage, click on **View Text**.

● iBT Practice 02

What Caused the Dinosaurs to Disappear?

Originally appearing about 230 million years ago, dinosaurs dominated the earth until they mysteriously vanished at the end of what is known as the Cretaceous period. It is estimated that they adapted well to their environment, reproducing freely and maintaining their position at the top of the food chain, so the reason why they suddenly became extinct 65 million years ago has become one of the more intriguing mysteries of paleontology. Many different theories have been 5 put forward as to the cause of dinosaur extinction.

➡ A belief among some scientists is that dinosaurs died out due to a series of giant volcanic eruptions. This theory suggests that tens of thousands of years of major volcanic eruptions resulted in huge dust clouds. ■ These blocked much of the sun's heat and light for long periods and resulted in a dramatic drop in temperatures and a reduction in photosynthetic activity in organisms like 10 marine plankton and land plants. ■ These organisms make up the bottom of the food chain, and changes at their level are magnified repeatedly when going up the chain. ■ Another view of the volcanic activity theory suggests large quantities of carbon dioxide were released by eruptions, causing global warming and acid rain that adversely affected the climate. ■ Support for this theory is provided by the largest series of volcanic eruptions in history, at the Deccan Traps in India, 15 happening at the estimated time of the dinosaur extinction.

➡ On the other hand, some scientists suggest that the dinosaurs finally became extinct due to a massive asteroid impact. In recent times, the impact theory has come in for wide-ranging support. It was first proposed in 1980 by Luis and Walter Alvarez. When they were making a study of the rocks around the K-T boundary, the thin clay layer that marks the boundary between the 20 Cretaceous and Tertiary rocks in Gubbio, Italy, they found a layer of clay at the boundary point that contained an unusually high amount of the rare element iridium. The levels of iridium contained in the clay were approximately 30 times the normal levels. Alvarez proposed that a sudden increase in iridium levels around 65.5 million years ago was direct evidence of an impact hit from some type of asteroid. Interestingly, a huge asteroid impact site was located in the Yucatán Peninsula, 25 Mexico, creating the 170 km-wide Chicxulub Crater, which could have triggered the mass extinction. Following such an impact, clouds of debris would have caused months of darkness and decreasing global temperatures. The effects would have been devastating, especially for dinosaurs, which needed large food supplies and sunlight to keep warm.

In the past few years, the scientific community, the media, and the general public have come 30 to support the impact theory of dinosaur extinction. It seems fairly certain from the large dinosaur graveyards that a major catastrophe occurred, but the truth about why this happened is still unexplained.

1. The word intriguing in the passage is closest in meaning to
   (A) rewarding   (B) fascinating   (C) enduring   (D) startling

2. Which of the sentences below best expresses the essential information in the highlighted sentence in the passage? *Incorrect* choices change the meaning in important ways or leave out essential information.
   (A) An alternative view is that serious climate change occurred due to volcanic eruptions.
   (B) An increase in volcanic activity resulted in huge amounts of acid rain, which had a negative impact on the climate.
   (C) Carbon dioxide caused by acid rain and global warming led to an environmental disaster.
   (D) Some volcanic theorists believe that catastrophic climate change was caused by volcanoes releasing huge amounts of carbon dioxide.

3. According to paragraph 2, the temperature dropped dramatically because
   (A) volcanic dust clouds blocked the heat from the sun
   (B) the amount of sunlight released from the sun decreased considerably
   (C) huge amounts of carbon dioxide were emitted by volcanic eruptions
   (D) acid rain led to a serious increase in the acidity of the seas
   Paragraph 2 is marked with an arrow [→].

4. Why does the author mention the Chicxulub Crater?
   (A) To explain why all dinosaurs in Mexico became extinct
   (B) To provide evidence of the asteroid impact theory
   (C) To illustrate how dust clouds traveled long distances
   (D) To identify the source of dinosaur fossils

5. What can be inferred from paragraph 3 about iridium?
   (A) Asteroids contain high amounts of iridium.
   (B) The level of iridium found in the clay indicates drastic weather change.
   (C) Iridium cannot be obtained in a natural state.
   (D) When the level of iridium increases, the environment becomes barren.
   Paragraph 3 is marked with an arrow [→].

6. Look at the four squares [■] that indicate where the following sentence could be added to the passage.

   The greatest effects are evident at the top among the larger predators and herbivores.

   Where would the sentence best fit?

   Click on a square [■] to add the sentence to the passage.

7. **Directions:** An introductory sentence for a brief summary of the passage is provided below. Complete the summary by selecting the THREE answer choices that express the most important ideas in the passage. Some sentences do not belong in the summary because they express ideas that are not presented in the passage or are minor ideas in the passage. *This question is worth 2 points.*

   Scientists have made efforts to explain the mystery of the dinosaur extinction.
   -
   -
   -

   Answer Choices

   (A) Recently, a group of scientists have argued that an asteroid impact triggered a mass extinction on Earth.

   (B) It took thousands of years for the dinosaurs to finally disappear from all the continents on Earth.

   (C) Some scientists suggest that an increase in volcanic activity led to catastrophic climate change.

   (D) Huge dust clouds led to the death of many animals, including dinosaurs.

   (E) Though the general public supports the impact theory, the truth remains hidden.

   (F) The levels of iridium contained in the K-T boundary were about 30 times the normal levels.

   Drag your answer choices to the spaces where they belong. To remove an answer choice, click on it. To review the passage, click on **View Text**.

Actual Practice Test

The Printing Press – a European Revolution

➡ Books were a scarce commodity in medieval Europe; the demand for texts existed, but the techniques used to produce books during this era did not allow for large numbers to be made. Up until the fourteenth century, all books were handwritten, copied laboriously from the original by a scribe. Often, the scribe would add intricate illustrations in and around the text, which increased the book's value. Book pages were made from stretched animal skin called vellum, an expensive 5 material. All of these factors contributed to the scarcity and high cost of books in the Middle Ages.

➡ Starting in the early 1300s, some European bookmakers adopted a technology from China called woodblock printing. Instead of writing out a page by hand, the text and illustration were carved into a piece of wood, covered with ink, and pressed onto a sheet of vellum. While woodblock printing eliminated the need for time-consuming hand copying of texts, it failed to 10 significantly increase the availability of books, for even though the woodblocks could be reused to print multiple copies of a text, the task of carving each letter and picture was tedious. Wood's lack of durability also limited the potential of this printing technique.

➡ Then, in around 1450, a German named Johannes Gutenberg transformed the printing industry forever through his pioneering work with the printing press, which employed moveable 15 type. Though it had been developed previously in other parts of the world, moveable type was perfected by Gutenberg, and his design was the archetype for all European printers who followed. First, he created metal type by casting the 26 letters of the Roman alphabet in lead, later attaching them to cylindrical metal punches that could be arranged in a printing plate, inked, and pressed onto a flat surface to create a page of text. For the next page, Gutenberg simply 20 had to rearrange the punches to form the desired words and sentences; the punches could be reused as long as the metal in which they were cast did not deteriorate. In addition, Gutenberg popularized the use of paper as a printing material and introduced durable oil-based printing inks, all of which culminated in a dramatic revolution in bookmaking in Europe.

➡ Within 50 years of the creation of the printing press, there were over a thousand printers 25 who had set up shops in over two hundred European cities. Gutenberg's invention allowed a single person to produce hundreds of copies of text a year, whereas the scribes of previous centuries had only been able to complete perhaps one book in a year. As books could be produced quickly and with relatively little effort, their price fell and more people were able to buy reading material. 30

➡ The growing presence of books in people's lives spurred an increase in adult literacy rates across Europe. Consequently, public demand increased for books on various topics and composed in languages other than Latin, which historically had been the linguistic standard for written works. Books were soon produced in the common European vernaculars, ultimately

leading to the decline of the Latin language. But even more important was the fact that 35
knowledge was now accessible to the ordinary person. New works of fiction, poetry, and history
appeared, and education levels steadily rose. In addition, the range of printed texts expanded
to include philosophical and scientific works of ancient Greece and Rome. ■ Up to this point,
European thinkers had relied heavily on Christian doctrine and the approval of the Church in
developing ideas about the world. ■ Now, with exposure to these classical points of view, 40
scholars throughout Europe began to adopt a more rational stance. ■ The result was a major
shift in thought, recognized today as the end of the Middle Ages and the commencement of the
Renaissance. ■

1. All of the following are mentioned in paragraph 1 as contributing to the scarcity and high cost of
    books EXCEPT
    Ⓐ a lack of scribes   Ⓑ inefficient production methods
    Ⓒ hand-drawn artistic additions   Ⓓ the use of a high-priced material
    Paragraph 1 is marked with an arrow [➡].

2. According to paragraph 2, which of the following is true about woodblock printing technology
    used in Europe in the fourteenth century?
    Ⓐ Letters were carved into a piece of wood.
    Ⓑ Paper was used in printing for the first time.
    Ⓒ It increased the popularity of books.
    Ⓓ The woodblock could not be reused.
    Paragraph 2 is marked with an arrow [➡].

3. Which of the sentences below best expresses the essential information in the highlighted
    sentence in the passage? *Incorrect* choices change the meaning in important ways or leave out
    essential information.
    Ⓐ The casting of letters out of lead was a key process in the creation of moveable type.
    Ⓑ The lead letters were attached to punches, and they could be arranged and inked to print
       pages.
    Ⓒ Gutenberg's printing press used lead letters which were specially organized to print pages.
    Ⓓ The surface that the 26 lead letters were pressed down onto had to be flat in order to be
       properly inked.

4. The phrase culminated in in the passage is closest in meaning to
   (A) held back   (B) reflected   (C) eliminated   (D) led to

5. In paragraph 3, the author states that Gutenberg's moveable type
   (A) set a standard in the printing industry
   (B) was perfected in other parts of the world
   (C) overshadowed the invention of the printing press
   (D) was not widely used until the late sixteenth century
   Paragraph 3 is marked with an arrow [➡].

6. In paragraph 4, how does the author explain the reason for the fast spread of the printing press?
   (A) By comparing the number of scribes with the number of printers
   (B) By noting the high demand for new texts at the time
   (C) By mentioning the profitability of the printing industry
   (D) By comparing the efficiency of the new and old methods
   Paragraph 4 is marked with an arrow [➡].

7. The phrase these classical points of view in the passage refers to
   (A) philosophical and scientific works of ancient Greece and Rome
   (B) Christian doctrine and the approval of the Church
   (C) Middle Ages
   (D) Renaissance

8. Why does the author mention rising literacy rates in paragraph 5?
   (A) To contrast the lower classes with the higher classes
   (B) To suggest a cause of the creation of the printing press
   (C) To show that Europeans were demanding a new culture
   (D) To identify an effect of Gutenberg's printing press
   Paragraph 5 is marked with an arrow [➡].

9. Look at the four squares [■] that indicate where the following sentence could be added to the passage.

> Furthermore, they could share their newly formulated theories and create communities for continuing discourse.

Where would the sentence best fit?

Click on a square [■] to add the sentence to the passage.

10. **Directions:** An introductory sentence for a brief summary of the passage is provided below. Complete the summary by selecting the THREE answer choices that express the most important ideas in the passage. Some sentences do not belong in the summary because they express ideas that are not presented in the passage or are minor ideas in the passage. **This question is worth 2 points.**

Before the 14th century, books in Europe were produced at a slow rate, keeping the supply low.

-
-
-

Answer Choices

(A) Over time, the printing press led to monumental changes in both the lives of common people and in the body of scholarly thought.

(B) Vellum was used instead of paper for both handwritten books and texts printed using the woodblock method.

(C) Gutenberg is usually credited with the invention of the first printing press, though earlier versions of the printing press existed in China.

(D) The introduction of woodblock printing offered a new bookmaking technique but was not revolutionary enough to affect the scarcity of texts.

(E) Once Gutenberg invented a printing press using moveable type, Europe became capable of mass-producing books.

(F) The first books produced by printing presses were similar in appearance to handwritten texts.

Drag your answer choices to the spaces where they belong. To remove an answer choice, click on it. To review the passage, click on **View Text**.

Organization

The Printing Press – a European Revolution

Before Gutenberg's printing press

- Books in the Middle Ages
  - Books were a rare and expensive commodity.
  - Each book had to be copied by _____ by a scribe.

- Woodblock printing
  - Was adopted from _____ in the early 1300s
  - Allowed for the printing of an entire page at a time
  - A lot of work was involved in _____ each woodblock.

Gutenberg's invention of a printing press with moveable type

- Moveable type printing press
  - Was invented by Johannes Gutenberg around 1450
  - Metal casts were made of each _____ of the alphabet.
  - Letters could be rearranged to create a new page of text.

- Advantages of Gutenberg's printing press
  - Allowed books to be produced much more _____ than before
  - Significantly brought down the _____ of books

- Effect of Gutenberg's printing press
  - Spread literacy throughout Europe
  - Allowed books to be printed in languages other than _____
  - Brought knowledge to the common people
  - Led to the beginning of the _____

Vocabulary Review

A **Fill in the blanks with the best answer. Change the form if necessary.**

angular	bud	ledge	cast	impulse	boast

1. The silversmith will _____ the molten metal into a mold, cool it, and then shape it.

2. The actor was easily remembered because of his sharp facial features, including a(n) _____ jaw.

3. Spring is characterized by newness of life – newly forming plant _____ and animal births.

4. Returning to her parents' home in the countryside sparked the author's creative _____.

5. The Henderson family decorated all their window _____ with flowerpots.

B **Choose the word or phrase that is closest in meaning to each highlighted word or phrase.**

1. It has been proven that a smell can effectively trigger a specific memory.
   - (A) erase
   - (B) command
   - (C) pass over
   - (D) activate

2. The politician reached the pinnacle of his career after winning the presidential election.
   - (A) height
   - (B) duration
   - (C) campaign
   - (D) preparation

3. Jack was confident that his friend's performance would not overshadow his own.
   - (A) disqualify
   - (B) discourage
   - (C) overestimate
   - (D) surpass

4. The virus, which has no cells, can't reproduce by itself and must replicate inside the living cells of an organism.
   - (A) feed
   - (B) survive
   - (C) multiply
   - (D) hide

5. Most teenagers subscribe to the belief that adults simply do not understand their world.
   - (A) reject
   - (B) support
   - (C) spread
   - (D) express

6. In Japan, plans have been completed for a solar-powered and self-contained city in a high-rise building.
   - (A) independent
   - (B) economic
   - (C) exceptional
   - (D) environment-friendly

7. The calm waters reflected a clear, inverted image of the old schoolhouse at the edge of the lake.
   - (A) unrealistic
   - (B) upside-down
   - (C) inside-out
   - (D) photographic

C **Choose the correct word in each sentence.**

1. When the dry winds blew, (petals, pebbles) turned brown before falling off.

2. If a farmer does not let the land rest, he risks it becoming (barren, barred) over time.

3. The famous scholar makes clear (disruptions, distinctions) between the four different types of love.

UNIT

Prose Summary

Vocabulary Preview

A **Choose the word that best matches each definition.**

> (A) penetrate   (B) incorporate   (C) salvation
>
> (D) emergence   (E) contour   (F) vibrate

1. to pass through or enter something: _____
2. protection from death, danger, or damage: _____
3. a gradual process of becoming visible: _____
4. the outline or shape of something, especially its surface: _____
5. to make short, quick movements back and forth or from side to side: _____

B **Choose the best synonym for each list of words.**

> (A) convention   (B) alternative   (C) skepticism   (D) complementary
>
> (E) flammable   (F) absurd   (G) neutral

1.	custom	tradition	practice	: _____
2.	unbiased	nonaligned	impartial	: _____
3.	doubt	uncertainty	suspicion	: _____
4.	substitute	option	replacement	: _____
5.	illogical	ridiculous	unreasonable	: _____
6.	interdependent	reciprocal	interrelating	: _____

C **Choose the right meaning for each highlighted word.**

1. Scientists want to develop a robot that analyzes sensory information correctly.
   (A) difficult to understand   (B) related to sight, sound, smell, touch, and taste

2. Sometimes, children have the most whimsical ideas and modes of expression.
   (A) sharply correct   (B) unusual and amusing

3. The passing of the summer heat and humidity made the area habitable again.
   (A) quiet and peaceful   (B) suitable or comfortable to live in

4. The student was able to answer even the most difficult questions quickly and definitively.
   (A) certainly or clearly   (B) too quickly to be accurate

5. Even though the new visitor was mysterious and quiet, the townspeople tried their best to embrace him.
   (A) to take in and accept someone   (B) to freely provide someone with food and shelter

08 Prose Summary

- Prose Summary questions test your ability to understand the whole passage and recognize the major ideas.
- An introductory sentence is provided and you must then select three of six choices that are most appropriate to complete the summary of the passage.
- Each reading passage contains either a Prose Summary or a Schematic Table question as the final question.
- Prose Summary questions are worth 2 points.
  (3 correct answers = 2 points / 2 correct answers = 1 point / 0 or 1 correct answers = 0 points)

Question Type

Directions: An introductory sentence for a brief summary of the passage is provided below. Complete the summary by selecting the THREE answer choices that express the most important ideas in the passage. Some sentences do not belong in the summary because they express ideas that are not presented in the passage or are minor ideas in the passage. *This question is worth 2 points.*

Drag your answer choices to the spaces where they belong. To remove an answer choice, click on it. To review the passage, click on **View Text**.

Strategy

1. Identify the main idea of the whole passage and locate the major ideas that support the main idea.
   - For each paragraph, make brief notes about the main idea. Topic sentences are usually located at the beginning or end of each paragraph.
   - Find the main idea by reading the given introductory sentence carefully as it is usually the topic sentence for the whole passage.

2. Eliminate incorrect choices to find the correct answer.
   - Try to eliminate those answer choices that are simply minor ideas or supporting details in the passage.
   - Try to eliminate those answer choices that are either not presented in the passage or contradict information presented in the passage.
   - The correct answer choices will bring major ideas together or paraphrase them.

Basic Drills

Sensation can be thought of as the passive process of bringing information into the body and brain from the outside by using sensory receptors. The eyes experience sensation when they collect rays of light and focus them on the retina. The ears feel sensation when waves of vibrating air are transferred from the outer ear through the middle ear to the auditory nerve.

Perception, on the other hand, is the process of actively selecting, organizing, and interpreting the information relayed to the brain by sensory receptors. For instance, the information sent to the retina may be interpreted as a color or shape, and those occurrences detected by the ear may be interpreted as musical sounds, a human voice, or some other noise.

Sensation begins when sensory receptors take in energy from the outside environment and then convert energy into neural impulses that are sent to the brain. As the brain organizes the information and makes something meaningful out of it, the process of perception commences. This complementary process of sensation and perception allows people to acquire external information and interact with it.

1

Directions: An introductory sentence for a brief summary of the passage is provided below. Complete the summary by selecting the THREE answer choices that express the most important ideas in the passage. Some sentences do not belong in the summary because they express ideas that are not presented in the passage or are minor ideas in the passage. ***This question is worth 2 points.***

The processes of sensation and perception are unique and separate from one another but operate in a complementary manner.

-
-
-

Answer Choices

Ⓐ Without the process of perception, the senses cannot detect information from the outside.

Ⓑ Sensation can be considered as the bringing in of information from the outside world by employing bodily organs.

Ⓒ Information sent to sensory receptors might arrive in the form of shapes and colors or sounds and vibrations.

Ⓓ When the brain gives meaning to the information provided by the senses, it begins the process of perception.

Ⓔ Perception relates to the act of choosing and understanding the information sent to the brain by the various senses.

Ⓕ In perception, the brain passively transmits information from the outside environment to the senses.

Drag your answer choices to the spaces where they belong. To remove an answer choice, click on it. To review the passage, click on **View Text**.

Dadaism is a cultural movement that began during World War I in Switzerland, which was neutral at that time. Although it is most well-known for visual arts, Dadaism also included literature, poetry and graphic design. The movement represented a protest against the World War and was therefore strongly opposed to the horror and destruction it produced. Dadaism was also a reaction against the foundations of modern European society and Western culture, including rationality, nationalism, and militarism, which its proponents felt were responsible for the advent of the World War. They reasoned that the philosophical, social, and cultural conventions of a society that could allow such large-scale destruction should be rebelled against and ultimately destroyed. Within a short time of promoting these views, it gained popularity and peaked between 1916 and 1920.

Dadaism sought salvation from the devastation of war by rejecting the logic that led to World War I and instead embraced anarchy and nihilism, rejecting established laws and institutions. It fought against the traditional standard of what is considered art and rejected conventional aesthetics through creating absurd and puzzling pieces. These acted as social and political statements rather than objects of beauty. The work that emerged out of this movement aimed to shock and challenge its audience in order to force them to question accepted aesthetic and artistic values. Ironically, however, this "anti-art" movement became an influential movement in modern art.

The movement was short-lived and declined in the early 1920s. Dadaism was superseded by surrealism, which shared many of the same characteristics, including irrationality and the element of surprise. Although Dadaism appeared to have died off, a revival occurred after World War II in the 1950s in New York. Since then, its legacy has been incorporated into the Pop Art movement, which utilized images from popular culture. The Dada movement was extremely influential on the development of twentieth-century art, so much so that its widespread innovations are taken for granted today.

Directions: An introductory sentence for a brief summary of the passage is provided below. Complete the summary by selecting the THREE answer choices that express the most important ideas in the passage. Some sentences do not belong in the summary because they express ideas that are not presented in the passage or are minor ideas in the passage. ***This question is worth 2 points.***

Dadaism was a reactionary cultural movement with its roots in the opposition to World War I.

-
-
-

Answer Choices

(A) The movement was a reaction to Western culture and its rationality, militarism, and nationalism.

(B) A revival of Dadaism surfaced in New York City in the 1950s for a few years.

(C) Though short-lived, Dadaism was extremely influential on twentieth-century art and thinking.

(D) It rejected the logic that led to the World War and challenged the traditional standards of art and aesthetics.

(E) Its artistic exhibits focused on beauty as well as on making social statements.

(F) Its popularity lasted until the late 1920s, when it was replaced by surrealism.

Drag your answer choices to the spaces where they belong. To remove an answer choice, click on it. To review the passage, click on **View Text**.

Due to a sharp rise in the popularity of billiards in the mid-nineteenth century in Europe and America, there was an increase in the demand for ivory which was used to manufacture billiard balls. However, over time the supply of ivory became insufficient to meet the demand, since so many elephants in Asia and Africa had been killed for their precious ivory. In order to fill this demand, a replacement for ivory needed to be found.   5

In 1863, the billiard ball company Phelan and Collander was offering a $10,000 reward to anybody who could invent a synthetic material to take the place of ivory in billiard balls. Motivated by the announcement, American printer John Wesley Hyatt began working on an alternative. He experimented with a substance called *collodion* as a substitute for ivory and in 1869 produced billiard balls using it. The solution was not complete, however, as the billiard balls made from   10 collodion shattered once they hit each other. To amend this, he added camphor, which comes from laurel trees, and mixed it with the collodion. Through this process, Hyatt finally succeeded in producing a smooth, hard, ivory-like substance and named it *celluloid*. However, Hyatt could not use celluloid to create billiard balls that were of the same quality as those made from ivory. Thus, he was never awarded the $10,000 prize.   15

Nevertheless, celluloid could be employed in many different areas, working as a substitute for ivory, tortoise shell, whalebone, and animal horn. Traditional products that had used these materials were much easier to fabricate with celluloid. With his brother Isaiah, Hyatt founded the Celluloid Manufacturing Company in 1871 and developed the necessary machinery for working celluloid. Afterwards, a wide range of items, including denture plates, collars and cuffs, knife   20 handles, combs, corsets, and even movie film were made of celluloid.

However, celluloid had several disadvantages which ultimately led to its decline. It was highly flammable and burned easily, which meant it was not a safe product to have in the house or around children. By the 1940s, it had largely been replaced by newer plastics, and these days, one of the few items made from celluloid are ping-pong balls.   25

1

Directions: An introductory sentence for a brief summary of the passage is provided below. Complete the summary by selecting the THREE answer choices that express the most important ideas in the passage. Some sentences do not belong in the summary because they express ideas that are not presented in the passage or are minor ideas in the passage. ***This question is worth 2 points.***

Because of the rise in the popularity of billiards and a downturn in the supply of ivory in the mid-nineteenth century, a synthetic substitute for ivory was necessary.

-
-
-

Answer Choices

Ⓐ A huge increase in the number of elephants being killed in Africa and Asia resulted in a substantial decrease in the availability of ivory.

Ⓑ The highly flammable nature of celluloid led to its downfall in favor of newer plastics by the 1940s.

Ⓒ Celluloid was used as a substitute for ivory, tortoise shell, whalebone, and animal horn because it was easy to manufacture.

Ⓓ After experimenting with collodion and camphor, Hyatt managed to produce a material very similar to ivory, which he called celluloid.

Ⓔ Though celluloid could not be used in billiard balls, it proved to be an efficient substitute in the production of various products.

Ⓕ After many experiments, Hyatt was able to produce a billiard ball that was as good as those made from ivory.

Drag your answer choices to the spaces where they belong. To remove an answer choice, click on it. To review the passage, click on **View Text**.

iBT Practice 01

Coral Reefs

→ The warm, shallow portions of the world's tropical oceans are home to some truly spectacular structures: coral reefs. These often enormous deposits of limestone are actually formed by colonies of living organisms known as stony corals. As stony corals live, grow, and die, they secrete calcium carbonate, which over time builds up to create the massive limestone reefs. However, certain conditions must exist for the corals to be able to survive and give rise to a reef. 5 The reef-building organisms cannot survive in water that is more than 55 meters deep because of their need for sunlight, and the temperature of the water must be above 18°C. Therefore, the most common location for a reef to grow is around a tropical island.

→ Coral reefs are separated into three general categories according to their structural characteristics in relation to the surrounding environment. Fringing reefs arise very close to an 10 island or other landmass, following the contours of the coastline and forming a border along the shore. Barrier reefs border landmasses in a similar fashion but are separated from the shore by a greater distance. Between the island and the reef is a lagoon, a calm body of water that can be quite deep. Finally, an atoll is a reef encircling a lagoon that has no central island protruding above the surface. Sand and other materials sometimes collect on top of an atoll to create a 15 brand-new island or islands, some of which become habitable for humans.

→ In the nineteenth century, the famous biologist Charles Darwin developed a theory that explained the three reef structures as steps in a process occurring over thousands of years. Central to this idea is the concept of island formation. Through volcanic activity from deep within the earth, new land is created and an island takes shape. Once the island has cooled enough to 20 support the presence of life, corals begin to grow in the surrounding shallow waters; as a result, fringing reefs take shape adjacent to the island's shoreline. Over millennia, the island begins to sink back beneath the ocean. As this happens, the coral continues to grow upward from its original position, usually at a speed that allows it to remain close to the surface. The result is the formation of a lagoon between the island and the coral – now a barrier reef. At some point, the 25 island will disappear completely, leaving only a circular atoll of coral surrounding a large lagoon.

Darwin's theory was strongly contested during the 1800s. In fact, it was not until 1951 that geologists were able to prove it definitively. They drilled holes and penetrated deep into the crust beneath Eniwetok, an atoll in the Pacific Ocean, where they found evidence of the old volcanic rock that had once been an island in the center of the circular reef. This discovery has enabled 30 scientists to better understand the complex and fascinating world of coral reefs.

1. Why does the author mention calcium carbonate?
   (A) To explain why stony corals live near islands
   (B) To list the main source of food for stony corals
   (C) To identify the material that coral reefs are composed of
   (D) To describe the environment where coral reefs are found

2. According to paragraph 1, coral reefs are mostly found around tropical islands because
   (A) these islands receive more sunlight than other places
   (B) water temperatures and depths are favorable there
   (C) food for reef-building organisms is sufficient there
   (D) they are protected from sudden changes in weather there
   Paragraph 1 is marked with an arrow [→].

3. The word protruding in the passage is closest in meaning to
   (A) moving   (B) extending   (C) sinking   (D) forming

4. According to paragraph 2, how are atolls different from fringing and barrier reefs?
   (A) They provide shelter for more species.
   (B) They form a border around a lagoon.
   (C) They are located close to an island.
   (D) They can transform into new islands.
   Paragraph 2 is marked with an arrow [→].

5. Based on information in paragraphs 1 and 3, why do corals grow upward when the island begins to sink?
   (A) They need to stay near the surface to receive sunlight.
   (B) They are prevented from growing inward because of the sinking island.
   (C) The sinking island lowers the temperature of the water around them.
   (D) They are forced upward by the lack of food in deep water.
   Paragraphs 1 and 3 are marked with arrows [→].

6. The word contested in the passage is closest in meaning to

   (A) disputed   (B) reinforced

   (C) believed   (D) developed

7. **Directions:** An introductory sentence for a brief summary of the passage is provided below. Complete the summary by selecting the THREE answer choices that express the most important ideas in the passage. Some sentences do not belong in the summary because they express ideas that are not presented in the passage or are minor ideas in the passage. **This question is worth 2 points.**

> Coral reefs, created by the growth of organisms called stony corals, can be found in many tropical oceans.
>
> •
>
> •
>
> •

Answer Choices

(A) Reef-building organisms cannot live in water that is more than 55 meters deep.

(B) There are three structural types of coral reefs, and each possesses different and unique characteristics.

(C) According to Darwin's theory, coral reefs begin to grow along an island's shoreline to form a fringing reef.

(D) Coral reefs are habitats for a variety of species in tropical oceans.

(E) Scientists were able to prove Darwin's theory by drilling below the surface of an atoll named Eniwetok.

(F) Darwin proposed that reef development progresses in phases, from fringing reef to barrier reef to atoll.

Drag your answer choices to the spaces where they belong. To remove an answer choice, click on it. To review the passage, click on **View Text**.

iBT Practice 02

The History of Weathervanes

Mentioned as far back as 3,500 years ago in the ancient writings of Mesopotamia, weathervanes are one of the oldest methods used to predict the weather. Weathervanes, sometimes referred to as *wind vanes*, derive their name from the Old English word *fane*, meaning a "flag" or "banner," as they were usually situated high up on a structure so as to catch the wind. Though they may not have been as accurate as modern scientific weather systems, these 5 ingenious devices helped to make predictions about climate trends.

➡ Weathervanes have a simple design, but in order to properly function, they need to follow two essential rules. First, they must be perfectly balanced on their rotating axis, meaning that half their weight sits on either side of the axis. Second, they must possess unequal surface area on each side that the wind can blow against. This causes the weathervane to rotate in order to 10 minimize the force of the wind on its surface, and as it rotates, the section with the smaller surface area turns into the wind, thereby signaling its direction. For a weathervane to operate efficiently it should be situated on the highest point of a building or structure; furthermore, it should be located away from other tall structures that may influence wind direction.

According to legend, the Greek astronomer Andronicus was responsible for the first "true 15 weathervane," a bronze structure placed atop the Tower of the Winds in Athens in 48 BC. This weathervane was between four and eight feet long and was shaped in the form of the Greek god Triton, who has the body of a man and the tail of a fish. The winds were thought by the ancient Greeks to possess divine powers, and weathervanes in the shape of various wind gods could be spied on the homes of wealthy landowners. By the ninth century AD, the Vikings were also 20 employing a type of weathervane to predict the weather. They created simple designs, made of bronze and other metals, which were often quadrant-shaped and depicted some creature from Norse mythology.

➡ In medieval Europe, a unique form of weathervane was commonly used. Noblemen flew banners and flags from castle towers, not to predict the weather but rather to help archers 25 calculate the direction of the wind when defending a castle. As time passed, the cloth flags were replaced by metal figures, and by the eighteenth and nineteenth centuries, weathervanes in Europe were being made with wrought iron. Around this time in England, the Victorians were manufacturing fascinating designs, with weathervanes serving as artistic expression, representing mythical creatures and animals. 30

Meanwhile, in the U.S., weathervanes gained fame following President George Washington's decision to erect one in the shape of a peace dove at his Mount Vernon home to commemorate the end of the Revolutionary War. Other patriotic symbols, such as the Federal Eagle and the Goddess of Liberty, also became popular with Americans after independence. As weathervanes

increased in popularity, American homeowners began to devise strange and whimsical designs. 35 Coastal residents enjoyed weathervanes shaped like ships, sea creatures, and other nautical themes. Additional popular designs included horses, wild animals, and angels.

1. Which of the sentences below best expresses the essential information in the highlighted sentence in the passage? *Incorrect* choices change the meaning in important ways or leave out essential information.

    (A) According to an Old English source, weathervanes need to be situated high off the ground in order to catch the wind.

    (B) Like flags and banners, weathervanes were typically located at the top of high structures.

    (C) The term *weathervane* comes from the Old English word for flag, a reference to the device's usual position.

    (D) The Old English term *fane* provided the basis for the modern name for the weathervane.

2. What can be inferred from paragraph 2 about weathervanes?

    (A) It is difficult to create a weathervane that functions properly.

    (B) In order to be functional, weathervanes cannot be decorative.

    (C) Weathervanes sometimes do not accurately indicate wind direction.

    (D) All working weathervanes share a similar design structure.

    Paragraph 2 is marked with an arrow [➡].

3. The word spied in the passage is closest in meaning to

    (A) included   (B) seen   (C) set   (D) made

4. According to paragraph 4, weathervanes in medieval Europe were unique in that they

    (A) took the form of flags and banners

    (B) were made of wrought iron

    (C) featured designs like gods and animals

    (D) were used as symbols of nobility

    Paragraph 4 is marked with an arrow [➡].

5. The word commemorate in the passage is closest in meaning to

    (A) expect   (B) assist   (C) announce   (D) honor

6. According to the passage, weathervanes have been used to do all of the following EXCEPT

   Ⓐ collect data about the weather

   Ⓑ express an artistic idea

   Ⓒ aid in military operations

   Ⓓ give thanks to a divine power

7. **Directions:** An introductory sentence for a brief summary of the passage is provided below. Complete the summary by selecting the THREE answer choices that express the most important ideas in the passage. Some sentences do not belong in the summary because they express ideas that are not presented in the passage or are minor ideas in the passage. ***This question is worth 2 points.***

> Weathervanes have been used for thousands of years as a means of predicting the weather.
>
> -
> -
> -

Answer Choices

Ⓐ From ancient Greece to medieval Europe, weathervanes were put to use for a variety of purposes.

Ⓑ The two halves of a weathervane are typically equal both in weight and surface area.

Ⓒ Because some Greek gods were associated with the wind, weathervanes were popular in that region.

Ⓓ There are specific design characteristics that a weathervane must possess if it is to work as desired.

Ⓔ Beginning in England and America, weathervanes came to take on artistic and patriotic representations.

Ⓕ The end of the Revolutionary War in the U.S. gave rise to many new styles of American weathervanes.

> Drag your answer choices to the spaces where they belong. To remove an answer choice, click on it. To review the passage, click on **View Text**.

Actual **Practice Test**

Miller and Urey's Model of the Origin of Life

➡ The nature of the origin of life has long been on the minds of scientists, and many thinkers have put forward theories about how life could have begun. In 1891, Charles Darwin suggested that the conditions on Earth when life first formed might have provided fertile grounds for the spontaneous emergence of life. He supposed that spontaneous generation could be tested in a laboratory setting, but the technological limitations of his time made such experiments   5
impossible. Until 1924, this theory about the origin of life remained relatively unchanged. It was further developed by Aleksandr Oparin, who proposed that life was a product of chemical evolution, originating with carbon-based molecules in the "primeval soup," the first oceans on Earth. Oparin's theory gained wide acceptance. In fact, it forms the basis of many current models of the origin of life. The oldest of these modern theories about the origin of life was put forth by   10
Stanley L. Miller and Harold C. Urey in 1953.

➡ Miller and Urey, scientists working with the University of Chicago, were curious about what specific environmental conditions on ancient Earth could have given rise to life. In the controlled setting of their laboratory, they attempted to recreate Earth's early environment, hoping to prove that life could arise in those conditions. Imitating what they believed to be the earth's   15
early atmosphere, they put methane, ammonia, hydrogen, and water into a sterile system of glass tubes and flasks. Next, to simulate the frequent lightning storms of the primitive planet, an electric current was supplied to the system. Within a few days, between 10 and 15 percent of the carbon had become organic compounds, and some of those organic compounds were amino acids, the basic units of life.   20

The results of Miller and Urey's experiment showed that amino acids could be fabricated relatively easily. This finding led to further research into the hypothetical origin of life on Earth. In the years after Miller and Urey's experiment, the scientific community was optimistic that the evidence provided by their work would soon lead to answers about the beginning of life.

➡ However, more than five decades after their notable experiment, these answers have   25
not yet materialized. In fact, Miller and Urey's experiment is now looked upon with skepticism by some. Questions have been raised about the accuracy with which their experiment simulated the conditions of early Earth. One problem is the continuous use of an electric current. Miller and Urey's experiment likely provided more energy than lightning storms on primitive Earth could have produced, for, although they were common, ancient lightning storms were not constant. Therefore,   30
it is unlikely that the amount of amino acids generated by Miller and Urey's system could have been created on the primitive planet. ■ Another problem with the 1953 experiment is the mixture of gases presumed to be the major components of the ancient atmosphere. ■ Since the time of Miller and Urey's experiment, a variety of alternative atmospheres have been proposed. ■

Scientists remain uncertain about the composition of the ancient atmosphere, and, consequently, 35 the validity of Miller and Urey's experiment remains in question. ■

1. The word **it** in the passage refers to
   (A) chemical evolution
   (B) primeval soup
   (C) Oparin's theory
   (D) wide acceptance

2. According to paragraph 1, Charles Darwin believed that
   (A) his hypothesis about the origin of life was impossible to test
   (B) spontaneous generation was an unrealistic hypothesis
   (C) organic molecules existed in a primeval soup on early Earth
   (D) the environment of ancient Earth might have been favorable to the creation of life
   Paragraph 1 is marked with an arrow [➡].

3. The word **sterile** in the passage is closest in meaning to
   (A) protected
   (B) unpolluted
   (C) transparent
   (D) complex

4. According to paragraph 2, all of the following are true of Miller and Urey's experiment EXCEPT
   (A) they tried to create a primitive environment in the controlled laboratory setting
   (B) methane, ammonia, hydrogen, and water were used to imitate the earth's early atmosphere
   (C) 10–15% of amino acids were compounded from carbon
   (D) they obtained organic compounds that act as the basic units of life within a few days
   Paragraph 2 is marked with an arrow [➡].

5. Based on information in paragraphs 1 and 2, what can be inferred about Miller and Urey's experiment?
   (A) It produced results that were completely unanticipated.
   (B) It supported Darwin's and Oparin's theories.
   (C) It was not considered influential at the time.
   (D) It troubled scientists who were skeptical of their work.
   Paragraphs 1 and 2 are marked with arrows [➡].

6. The word fabricated in the passage is closest in meaning to
   (A) increased
   (B) operated
   (C) produced
   (D) transferred

7. Which of the sentences below best expresses the essential information in the highlighted sentence in the passage? *Incorrect* choices change the meaning in important ways or leave out essential information.
   (A) In their experiment, Miller and Urey had to find a way to supply energy that would correspond to the energy provided by lightning storms.
   (B) While lightning storms on ancient Earth were frequent, they were relatively weak and rarely provided much energy.
   (C) Miller and Urey's experiment required energy because ancient Earth experienced frequent, though perhaps not continuous, lightning storms.
   (D) Miller and Urey's experiment probably supplied more energy than lightning storms on ancient Earth did.

8. Why does the author mention lightning storms and atmospheric gases in paragraph 4?
   (A) To demonstrate that there are a variety of theories about the origin of life
   (B) To justify Miller and Urey's use of an electric current
   (C) To suggest that Miller and Urey's conclusions may not be accurate
   (D) To explain why few have pursued work like Miller and Urey's
   Paragraph 4 is marked with an arrow [➡].

9. Look at the four squares [■] that indicate where the following sentence could be added to the passage.

   Some of these alternative theories speculate that oxygen might have been a major component in the earth's atmosphere, which would drastically change the results of the experiment.

   Where would the sentence best fit?

   Click on a square [■] to add the sentence to the passage.

10. **Directions:** An introductory sentence for a brief summary of the passage is provided below. Complete the summary by selecting the THREE answer choices that express the most important ideas in the passage. Some sentences do not belong in the summary because they express ideas that are not presented in the passage or are minor ideas in the passage. ***This question is worth 2 points.***

> Miller and Urey's experiment represented an important advancement in science's quest for answers about the origin of life.
>
> -
> -
> -

Answer Choices

Ⓐ Darwin thought that life might have arisen spontaneously on Earth.

Ⓑ Miller and Urey's experiment was based on ideas about the conditions on ancient Earth that were proposed by earlier scientists.

Ⓒ By simulating the earth's early environment, Miller and Urey demonstrated that it could have given rise to organic molecules.

Ⓓ After Miller and Urey completed their experiment, other scientists were encouraged to hypothesize about how life on Earth may have begun.

Ⓔ Miller and Urey used an electric current to simulate primitive lightning storms.

Ⓕ Miller and Urey's experiment has yet to be validated because of the uncertainty over the amount of energy available on ancient Earth and the planet's early atmosphere.

Drag your answer choices to the spaces where they belong. To remove an answer choice, click on it. To review the passage, click on **View Text**.

Organization

Miller and Urey's Model of the Origin of Life

Early theories about the origin of life

- _____ _____: life was spontaneously generated on Earth
- Oparin's theory: life chemically evolved from the "_____ _____" that was Earth's first oceans

Miller and Urey's experiment

① Purpose: to recreate the conditions that led to the beginnings of life on ancient Earth

② Conditions of early Earth

- Atmosphere: combined _____, ammonia, hydrogen, and water in test tubes
- Lightning: used a(n) _____ _____ to simulate lightning storms
- Result: creation of _____ _____, the building blocks of life

Effect of Miller and Urey's experiment

- Led to further research on the origins of life
- Scientists' optimistic view that the origins of life would soon be revealed

Criticism of Miller and Urey's experiment

- Constant electric current provided more energy than _____ _____ would have.
- Assumption of the composition of the _____ _____ could be wrong.

Vocabulary Review

A **Fill in the blanks with the best answer. Change the form if necessary.**

devastation	reactionary	divine	amend	weathervane	archer

1. In his opinion, Congress did not try hard enough to _____ the law.
2. Louis the Fourteenth firmly believed that he had the _____ right to rule France.
3. Pushing oneself to work too much can result in physical and emotional _____.
4. The _____ were given the command to shoot some time after the foot soldiers had been sent out.
5. Whereas weather stations are equipped with highly sophisticated instruments for studying the wind, the average man has just a(n) _____ on his roof.

B **Choose the word that is closest in meaning to each highlighted word.**

1. They erected a bronze statue in memory of the war hero.
   - Ⓐ designed Ⓑ built Ⓒ purchased Ⓓ decorated

2. The advent of industrialization introduced convenience as well as pollution.
   - Ⓐ adaptation Ⓑ passing Ⓒ arrival Ⓓ development

3. The use of e-mail has superseded the use of the letter as the major form of written communication.
   - Ⓐ popularized Ⓑ promoted Ⓒ outperformed Ⓓ replaced

4. The baseball flew out of the park and shattered the window of a neighboring house.
   - Ⓐ broke Ⓑ knocked Ⓒ shook Ⓓ passed

5. Proper protection must be worn at all times when handling this chemical compound.
   - Ⓐ ingredient Ⓑ cleaner Ⓒ mixture Ⓓ poison

6. Mr. Grey is the manager of a factory where the workers manufacture computers.
   - Ⓐ produce Ⓑ analyze Ⓒ repair Ⓓ transport

7. The customer was talking non-stop and appeared to have lost all rationality.
   - Ⓐ happiness Ⓑ reasoning Ⓒ shock Ⓓ humor

C **Choose the correct word in each sentence.**

1. Players (comment, commence) training even before the soccer season starts.
2. Less expensive material is often used to (simulate, stimulate) wood in cheap furniture.
3. It is the responsibility of this government office to check the (validity, solidity) of all information submitted on application forms.

Schematic Table

Vocabulary Preview

A **Choose the word that best matches each definition.**

> Ⓐ chord   Ⓑ heritage   Ⓒ potter   Ⓓ basin
>
> Ⓔ decorate   Ⓕ circumnavigate

1. to travel around the world in a ship: _____
2. to make attractive by adding fancy adornments: _____
3. three or more musical notes sounded in harmony: _____
4. a person who makes decorative ware using clay and a wheel: _____
5. tradition that is passed down through generations: _____

B **Choose the best synonym for each list of words.**

> Ⓐ nonsensical   Ⓑ identical   Ⓒ facilitate   Ⓓ ornament
>
> Ⓔ merge   Ⓕ fragment   Ⓖ expedition

1. scrap	piece	bit	: _____
2. same	alike	twin	: _____
3. beautify	adorn	decorate	: _____
4. combine	blend	mix	: _____
5. senseless	illogical	silly	: _____
6. promote	aid	expedite	: _____

C **Choose the right meaning for each highlighted word.**

1. He saw dense smoke rising from one of the buildings.
   - Ⓐ thick in concentration
   - Ⓑ completely free of

2. Bacteria multiply rapidly in food left in temperatures between 40°F and 140°F.
   - Ⓐ to become active
   - Ⓑ to increase greatly in number

3. The patient began to panic as the dressing that covered the lesion on his arm turned red.
   - Ⓐ a well-defined site of injury
   - Ⓑ muscles and bones

4. The immigrant family on the ship dreamed of finally reaching America, the land of abundance.
   - Ⓐ freedom and justice
   - Ⓑ plenty of food and money

5. The writer's final version of the story evolved from three different drafts of different stories.
   - Ⓐ to develop
   - Ⓑ to cut and paste

09 Schematic Table

Introduction

- Schematic Table questions test whether you are able to accurately categorize key information from the passage.
- The maximum points for this question type is either 3 or 4.
  ① When required to select 7 answers out of 9 choices:
    7 correct answers = 4 points / 6 correct answers = 3 points / 5 correct answers = 2 points / 4 correct answers = 1 point / 3 or fewer correct answers = 0 points
  ② When required to select 5 answers out of 7 choices:
    5 correct answers = 3 points / 4 correct answers = 2 points
    3 correct answers = 1 point / 2 or fewer correct answers = 0 points

Question Type

Directions: Complete the table by matching the phrases/statements below. Select the appropriate phrases/statements from the answer choices and match them to the category to which they relate. TWO of the answer choices will NOT be used. *This question is worth 3(4) points.*

> Drag your answer choices to the spaces where they belong. To remove an answer choice, click on it. To review the passage, click on **View Text**.

Strategy

1. A Schematic Table question is likely to be presented when the passage is organized in the following ways: compare-contrast, problem-solution, or cause-effect. Therefore, categorize important information while reading the passage.

2. Identify the key word/phrase of an answer choice in the passage and scan the surrounding information.

3. Become familiar with the characteristics of correct and incorrect answers.
   - Correct answers contain either paraphrased information from the passage or comprehensive information from several sentences.
   - Incorrect answers contain the following characteristics:
     ① Information not presented in the passage
     ② Incorrect descriptions of information from the passage
     ③ Information presented in the passage but irrelevant to the category in question

Basic Drills

A warm-blooded animal that controls its body temperature by generating heat through its own metabolism is known as an endotherm. Such a being possesses internal mechanisms that can regulate body temperature, usually above the temperature of its surrounding environment. Birds and mammals are examples of endotherms. In contrast, an ectotherm is a cold-blooded animal that uses the temperature of the outside environment to control its body temperature instead of producing enough of its own body heat. It regulates body temperature by moving from shaded to exposed areas. Creatures such as fish, amphibians, and reptiles are ectotherms.

Endotherms have higher metabolic rates. This means they require more energy to power the basic functions that are necessary to support life – for example, cell maintenance, breathing, and heartbeat. They also have higher temperature regulation costs to keep their body temperature at warm levels. On the other hand, the metabolic rates and the temperature regulation costs of ectotherms are comparatively low. In general, endotherms require 5 to 10 times as much food as ectotherms of the same size and build in order to maintain their metabolisms at the required rate. Thus, endotherms have to spend a lot more time searching for food to eat, while ectotherms can have one meal and survive for weeks.

1

Directions: Complete the table by matching the phrases below. Select the appropriate phrases from the answer choices and match them to the type of animals to which they relate. TWO of the answer choices will NOT be used. *This question is worth 3 points.*

Drag your answer choices to the spaces where they belong. To remove an answer choice, click on it. To review the passage, click on **View Text**.

Answer Choices	Endotherm
(A) Has a metabolism that operates at a high rate (B) Keeps body temperature higher than that of surrounding environment (C) Controls body heat by moving in and out of shaded areas (D) Requires a lot of energy to keep the same temperature as its surroundings	▶ ▶ ▶
(E) Controls body temperature by eating less (F) Contains an internal process that regulates body temperature (G) Incurs low costs in relation to temperature regulation	Ectotherm ▶ ▶

● Reading Practice 01

During the nineteenth century, breakthroughs were made concerning the correlation between the left hemisphere of the brain and language. Neurologists Paul Broca and Carl Wernicke undertook research in this area and found that people who had damage to a certain region in the left hemisphere of the brain had difficulties with speech and language. They observed that people who suffered injuries to the same area in the right hemisphere did not, however, experience any difficulty with language. This led them to conclude that the left hemisphere controls language function.

In 1861, Broca worked with a patient who could understand everything said to him but could only articulate one word: "tan." Subsequently, the man was given the same nickname. When Broca carried out an autopsy on Tan's brain after his death, he found a large lesion in the left frontal cortex of his brain. After studying eight other patients who presented the same speech problem, he was led to conclude that this part of the brain is responsible for creating speech. From then on, this section of the brain has been referred to as Broca's area. Those who suffer from Broca's aphasia can understand language but cannot speak at all, or, if they can, their speech is impaired.

In 1873, Wernicke discovered that injury to a different part of the brain was also responsible for causing language problems. This area, termed Wernicke's area, was also in the left hemisphere but it was positioned closer to the back of the brain and lower than Broca's area. While Broca's area is responsible for speech production, Wernicke's area is responsible for speech comprehension, and damage to this region causes Wernicke's aphasia, the loss of the ability to understand language. Sufferers of Wernicke's aphasia can speak normally, but their speech is nonsensical, incoherent, and littered with grammatical errors.

Glossary

aphasia: a disease characterized by loss of the ability to speak

1

Directions: Complete the table by matching the phrases below. Select the appropriate phrases from the answer choices and match them to the type of brain areas to which they relate. TWO of the answer choices will NOT be used. *This question is worth 3 points.*

> Drag your answer choices to the spaces where they belong. To remove an answer choice, click on it. To review the passage, click on **View Text**.

Answer Choices	Broca's area
(A) Is related to speech comprehension	▶
(B) Is related to speech production	▶
(C) Is in the left frontal cortex of the brain	**Wernicke's area**
(D) Is related to word memorization	▶
(E) Is responsible for controlling speech speed	▶
(F) Is in the back left section of the brain	▶
(G) Is responsible for speaking without grammatical errors	

Extra Question

The word articulate in the passage is closest in meaning to

(A) memorize

(B) prefer

(C) catch

(D) pronounce

The potters of ancient Greece were fortunate to have an abundance of quality clay. Around Athens, the local clay had a distinctive reddish-orange color because of its iron oxide content. With this hued clay, artists who decorated Greek pottery developed two decorative styles: the black-figure style and the red-figure style.

The black-figure style of pottery decoration emerged in Corinth around the seventh century 5 BC. Vase painters decorated bare pottery using a fluid form of clay called slip, which turned black when fired in a kiln. With this slip, artists painted narrative scenes featuring black figures in the foreground. The figures were essentially silhouettes, and details within the silhouetted figures were incised before firing. Against the orange backdrop of the clay, the contrast of these black silhouettes was quite striking. Orange and black were the dominant colors in these compositions, 10 but they were not the only colors used by artists of the black-figure style. Red and white were used as accent colors to ornament the simple black figures.

Red-figure pottery, which was developed in Athens around 530 BC, totally transformed the appearance of Greek pottery and soon superseded black-figure pottery as the style of preference for vase painting. This style was the opposite of the black-figure style; the figures were 15 left unpainted while the surface of the vase outside the figures was painted black. A fine brush was used to add details, applying black slip to enhance the figures. Various metals including gold were added to embellish details, whereas secondary colors of red and white were used less frequently. A more naturalistic and aesthetically pleasing treatment of human figures was facilitated by the red-figure style. The red shades mimicked the color and tone of sun-bronzed 20 skin and dramatically highlighted the figures against the dark background. Compared to the incising of the black-figure style, detailed painting with the brush led to greater flexibility in representing human form, movement, expressions, and perspective.

Directions: Complete the table by matching the phrases below. Select the appropriate phrases from the answer choices and match them to the type of pottery styles to which they relate. TWO of the answer choices will NOT be used. *This question is worth 3 points.*

Drag your answer choices to the spaces where they belong. To remove an answer choice, click on it. To review the passage, click on **View Text**.

Answer Choices	Black-figure style
Ⓐ Originated with pottery painters in Corinth	▶
Ⓑ First appeared during the eighth century BC	▶
Ⓒ Provided artists with a relatively realistic skin tone for figures	**Red-figure style**
Ⓓ Incised details within the silhouetted figures	▶
Ⓔ Did not make use of black slip	▶
Ⓕ Used gold to decorate the details of figures	▶
Ⓖ Came into use around the year 530 BC	

Extra Question

The word embellish in the passage is closest in meaning to

Ⓐ produce

Ⓑ adorn

Ⓒ emphasize

Ⓓ feature

iBT Practice 01

The Birth of Jazz

→ Jazz music represents a coming together of many different people and their heritages to produce a unique and multifaceted form of music. Its roots can be traced back to the 1880s and the merging of African musical influences with Western European music. The music of black slaves in the plantations took the form of work songs whose harmonic, rhythmic, and melodic elements were mostly African. These blended with the European-American musical heritage, which was composed of brass instruments such as trumpets and saxophones as well as the harmonic structures created by European composers. This unique blend created the foundation for ragtime, blues, and other musical genres from which jazz evolved.

→ Ragtime was one of the early styles of music to contribute to the development of jazz. Composed primarily for solo piano, ragtime mixed a sixteenth-note-based syncopated melody with the atmosphere of a march. This sound was achieved when the pianist's left hand played a "boom-chic" bass and chord pattern while the right hand played the syncopated tune. This style of music was called "ragging," and this is most likely where the term "ragtime" is derived from. With its complex rhythms, ragtime gleaned inspiration from other European musical forms such as the waltz and the polka combined with dance music like the "cakewalk." Ragtime was still not yet jazz as it did not really swing or improvise, but its popularity and influence grew with stars such as Scott Joplin.

Blues music was just as influential as ragtime in the development of jazz. Though blues music has no direct ancestors in European or African music, it was the stories and emotions of African-American oral tradition from the 1860s that formed the basis of blues. This tradition blended with European musical traditions and developed by emphasizing improvisation. Its unique tonal coloration became an important part of the jazz vocabulary and the most recognizable vocal style in jazz.

→ Ragtime and blues came together in New Orleans in the early 1920s, along with a rich local brass band tradition, to create a new form of jazz called Dixieland. These small bands were comprised of a brass section that usually included trumpet, clarinet, and trombone as well as a rhythm section made up of bass, drums, guitar, and on occasion, piano. This style used more intricate rhythms than ragtime and included various blues-style elements, all played in a novel, upbeat way on European instruments. Also named traditional jazz or New Orleans jazz, Dixieland soon spread from New Orleans to the major jazz centers of Chicago, New York, and Kansas City.

1. In paragraph 1, the author mentions all of the following as contributing to the development of ragtime, blues, and jazz EXCEPT
   - (A) using traditional African instruments
   - (B) characteristics of European composition
   - (C) African American slave music
   - (D) the European-American musical tradition

   Paragraph 1 is marked with an arrow [➡].

2. The word gleaned in the passage is closest in meaning to
   - (A) noted
   - (B) offered
   - (C) gathered
   - (D) used

3. The author discusses ragtime music in paragraph 2 by
   - (A) giving a technical description of its style
   - (B) contrasting it with the blues music tradition
   - (C) naming the best-known songs from the genre
   - (D) listing important features that influenced blues

   Paragraph 2 is marked with an arrow [➡].

4. Compared to ragtime, blues music places emphasis on
   - (A) European musical traditions
   - (B) the skill of improvising
   - (C) a technique called swing
   - (D) the use of the solo piano

5. The word intricate in the passage is closest in meaning to
   - (A) spontaneous
   - (B) sympathetic
   - (C) popular
   - (D) complex

6. What can be inferred from paragraph 4 about New Orleans?

　Ⓐ Most famous brass musical instruments were manufactured there.

　Ⓑ It was a musically active city before the introduction of jazz.

　Ⓒ Many of the earliest jazz musicians were born there.

　Ⓓ It was larger than Chicago, New York, and Kansas City in the early 1920s.

　Paragraph 4 is marked with an arrow [➔].

7. **Directions:** Complete the table by matching the phrases below. Select the appropriate phrases from the answer choices and match them to the type of music to which they relate. TWO of the answer choices will NOT be used. *This question is worth 3 points.*

> Drag your answer choices to the spaces where they belong. To remove an answer choice, click on it. To review the passage, click on **View Text**.

Answer Choices	Ragtime
Ⓐ Was influenced by waltz and polka	▶
Ⓑ Failed to gain in popularity because of its complex rhythms	▶
Ⓒ Was influenced by African American stories and emotions	▶
Ⓓ Required a brass section and a rhythm section	**Blues**
Ⓔ Contributed to a vocal style of jazz music	▶
Ⓕ Was most commonly played on the piano	▶
Ⓖ Made use of syncopation in the melody	

iBT Practice 02

Asexual Reproduction

Asexual reproduction is the primary form of reproduction in those species that do not include separate male and female life-forms. Reproduction among single-celled organisms, as well as among some plants and fungi, involves replication and not the manufacture and fusion of sex cells from two parents as is necessary in sexual reproduction. Because of this, asexual reproduction occurs much faster than sexual reproduction and requires less energy. Under ideal conditions, as each member of the population is capable of bearing young, an asexual population will grow twice as quickly as a sexual population half made up of males.

➔ One of the most common methods of asexual reproduction consists of a process known as "binary fission." Bacteria and amoeba are two organisms that reproduce asexually through binary fission. Both of these organisms use a simple method of asexual reproduction – they divide in half, producing two smaller daughter cells, using a process called fission. It results in the separation of a single cell into two identical daughter cells each containing a copy of the parental DNA. In turn, these two daughter cells divide in half following a time of feeding and growth. Provided that there are adequate nutrients, organisms reproducing via binary fission can multiply into billions or more relatively quickly.

Another common form of asexual reproduction is known as "budding." In this form, a daughter cell grows out of the body of a mother cell. One such example is the hydra, which develops a swelling on the side of its body that grows into a daughter bud. After a while, this daughter grows tentacles and starts catching small water animals for food. At this point, it separates from the mother hydra and drifts until it lands on a support.

Another way to reproduce asexually wherein the parent breaks into different fragments, which eventually form new individuals, is termed "fragmentation." These fragments develop into mature, fully grown individuals that are clones of the original organism. A typical example among animals is the flatworm.

➔ Many forms of asexual reproduction produce an exact clone of the parent, and this may prove advantageous if the genotype is well-suited to a stable environment as asexual reproduction allows beneficial combinations of genetic traits to remain unchanged. In addition, it eliminates problematic stages of early embryonic growth where the mixing of genes can cause problems such as mutation. However, the fact that offspring produced by asexual reproduction do not have any genetic variation can also be a disadvantage because as general variability decreases, a population is less able to develop new characteristics in order to adapt to and survive changes in an environment.

1. The word replication in the passage is closest in meaning to
   (A) renovation
   (B) splitting
   (C) copying
   (D) expansion

2. Why does the author mention the manufacture and fusion of sex cells?
   (A) To illustrate the difference between asexual and sexual reproduction
   (B) To define the necessary conditions for asexual reproduction
   (C) To identify the benefits of asexual reproduction
   (D) To provide an example of the most efficient type of reproduction

3. Which of the sentences below best expresses the essential information in the highlighted sentence in the passage? *Incorrect* choices change the meaning in important ways or leave out essential information.
   (A) An asexual population will increase at double the rate of a sexual one consisting of 50% males because the entire population is capable of giving birth.
   (B) If the conditions are ideal, an asexual population will grow at twice the rate of a sexual population because they are made up of 50% males.
   (C) Because males make up 50% of a sexual population, such a population will grow at different speeds depending on the conditions of the environment.
   (D) Sexual populations are more efficient at reproducing because they are made up of 50% females, which can give birth to young.

4. According to paragraph 2, which of the following is NOT true about binary fission?
   (A) One organism divides in half to reproduce.
   (B) Each daughter cell has the same DNA as its parents.
   (C) Organisms can only separate one time.
   (D) Organisms can rapidly reproduce using this method.
   Paragraph 2 is marked with an arrow [→].

5. The word it in the passage refers to
   (A) mother cell
   (B) body
   (C) daughter
   (D) food

6. In paragraph 5, which of the following is mentioned as a disadvantage of asexual reproduction?

   Ⓐ Spread of unchanged harmful genetic traits

   Ⓑ Early embryonic stages that cause mutation

   Ⓒ Less chance of surviving environmental changes

   Ⓓ Excessive genetic variation from multiple reproduction

Paragraph 5 is marked with an arrow [➡].

7. **Directions:** Complete the table by matching the statements below. Select the appropriate statements from the answer choices and match them to the type of asexual reproduction to which they relate. TWO of the answer choices will NOT be used. ***This question is worth 3 points.***

> Drag your answer choices to the spaces where they belong. To remove an answer choice, click on it. To review the passage, click on **View Text**.

Answer Choices	Binary fission
Ⓐ The hydra is one example of this reproduction method. ▶	
Ⓑ The pieces of flatworms grow into mature individual organisms. ▶	
Ⓒ The daughter cell grows from a swelling on the side of the parent cell.	**Budding**
Ⓓ Bacteria and amoeba use this method of asexual reproduction. ▶	
Ⓔ Cells split apart and rejoin to create a new organism. ▶	
Ⓕ Mutation might be caused by this method.	**Fragmentation**
Ⓖ Daughter cells continue to reproduce by dividing in half in rapid reproduction. ▶	

Actual Practice Test

Expeditions to Venus

→ Humans have been familiar with Venus since prehistoric times due to it being the brightest object in the sky apart from the Sun and the moon. With the invention of modern astronomical instruments, astronomers continued to observe Venus from Earth for centuries. However, because of its thick layer of dense clouds, it was difficult to observe the surface of Venus even with these new technologies. To overcome this difficulty and acquire information on Venus, a series of missions to explore the planet began in the 1960s.

On August 27, 1962, the interplanetary spacecraft known as Mariner 2 was launched into space by the U.S. Approaching Venus within about 21,607 miles, it transmitted coded signals continuously to Earth along the way, combining scientific data on interplanetary dust, magnetism, cosmic rays, and solar plasma with engineering data on the spacecraft's condition and performance. The major discoveries made by Mariner 2 were that Venus experienced a slow retrograde rotation rate, high surface pressures, hot surface temperatures, and no detectable magnetic field. In addition, it was found that the solar wind streams all the time in interplanetary space and the cosmic dust density is at a much lower level than that of near-Earth regions.

→ The Soviet Union also participated in the exploration of Venus. The Venera missions were a series of unmanned expeditions to Venus. The first few Venera missions met with mixed success, and it was Venera 4 in 1967 that gave science its first direct measurements for a model of Venusian atmospheric makeup. On August 17, 1970, the Soviet Union launched Venera 7, and on December 15, 1970, it became the first probe ever to successfully land on the surface of another planet. For 23 minutes, Venera 7 transmitted data indicating a surface temperature of 475°C and a surface pressure at 90 bar, which is equivalent to that found 0.6 miles beneath the ocean. In 1975, the first craft to orbit Venus, Venera 9 and 10, relayed back the first close-up photographs of the surface of the planet. These images revealed that some areas of Venus are covered with sharp-edged rocks while others contain fine-grained dust.

American Pioneer Venus 1 and Pioneer Venus 2 began orbiting the planet in December 1978. ■ Data from the radar mapper resulted in scientists being able to produce a topographical map of most of the surface of Venus between 73° north and 63° south latitude. ■ The findings suggested that Venus is much smoother than Earth, but that it has enormous mountains and deep basins on its surface. ■ Furthermore, the orbiter managed to identify the highest point on Venus as Maxwell Montes, which rises 10.8 kilometers above the average surface. ■

→ Named in honor of the sixteenth-century Portuguese navigator who was the first to lead an expedition that circumnavigated Earth, Magellan was launched on May 4, 1989 by the U.S., and entered into an orbit of Venus on August 10, 1990. Magellan gathered radar images of 84 percent of the Venusian surface. Venus was found to have millions of volcanoes, but unlike on

Earth, they were distributed randomly around the planet. Moreover, lava channels measuring 35 over 6,000 kilometers in length evidenced that lava probably erupted from these volcanoes in enormous quantities.

1. According to paragraph 1, what prevented humans from viewing the surface of Venus?
   - Ⓐ Its long distance from Earth
   - Ⓑ Insufficient technology
   - Ⓒ A thick layer of cloud cover
   - Ⓓ Its proximity to the Sun

   Paragraph 1 is marked with an arrow [➡].

2. Which of the sentences below best expresses the essential information in the highlighted sentence in the passage? *Incorrect* choices change the meaning in important ways or leave out essential information.
   - Ⓐ It transmitted data related to magnetism and cosmic rays back to Earth from its flight path as it came close to Venus.
   - Ⓑ It gathered significant data on the Venusian atmosphere after checking its own condition.
   - Ⓒ It analyzed scientific data on the spacecraft's performance as it approached within 21,607 miles of Venus.
   - Ⓓ It regularly sent messages concerning scientific and engineering data back to Earth as it came within 21,607 miles of Venus.

3. The word detectable in the passage is closest in meaning to
   - Ⓐ evident
   - Ⓑ adequate
   - Ⓒ powerful
   - Ⓓ permanent

4. The word its in the passage refers to
   - Ⓐ Venus
   - Ⓑ success
   - Ⓒ Venera 4
   - Ⓓ science

VOLUME   HELP   OK   NEXT

5. The word probe in the passage is closest in meaning to
    (A) machine   (B) evidence
    (C) explorer   (D) planet

6. According to paragraph 3, what can be inferred about Venera missions before 1967?
    (A) They provided information on Venusian surface temperature and pressure.
    (B) They managed to take the first pictures of the surface of Venus.
    (C) They were not successful because of their pilots' lack of experience.
    (D) Some of them failed to completely achieve their goals.
    Paragraph 3 is marked with an arrow [➡].

7. According to paragraph 5, Magellan found that numerous volcanoes on Venus
    (A) were distributed without any regular pattern
    (B) were much bigger than those found on Earth
    (C) were the sources of small amounts of lava
    (D) were sometimes more than 6,000 kilometers in length
    Paragraph 5 is marked with an arrow [➡].

8. In the passage, in what order does the author explain a series of expeditions to Venus?
    (A) From the U.S. to the Soviet Union expeditions
    (B) From the earliest to the latest expedition
    (C) From the longest to the shortest expedition
    (D) From the most important to the least important expedition

9. Look at the four squares [■] that indicate where the following sentence could be added to the passage.

    Their objectives were to orbit Venus for a lengthy period and map its surface using a radar package.

    Where would the sentence best fit?

    Click on a square [■] to add the sentence to the passage.

10. **Directions:** Complete the table by matching the phrases below. Select the appropriate phrases from the answer choices and match them to the findings by the U.S. and the Soviet Union spacecrafts to which they relate. TWO of the answer choices will NOT be used. ***This question is worth 4 points.***

> Drag your answer choices to the spaces where they belong. To remove an answer choice, click on it. To review the passage, click on **View Text**.

Answer Choices	Findings of U.S. spacecrafts
(A) Measurements for the atmospheric makeup of Venus	▶
(B) Venus having traces of volcanic eruptions	▶
(C) First unmanned expedition	▶
(D) A lower level of cosmic dust density in interplanetary space	▶
(E) Venus having huge basins on its surface	**Findings of Soviet spacecrafts**
(F) Venus experiencing weather patterns different from Earth	▶
(G) Exact Venusian surface temperature and pressure measurements	▶
(H) Venus being home to fine dust and sharp rocks depending on the area	▶
(I) Venus having a slow retrograde rotation rate	

Organization

Expeditions to Venus

Introduction

Astronomers on Earth have been observing Venus for hundreds of years.

A series of Venus exploration

① The Mariner missions (U.S.)

— Mariner 2 passed in close proximity to Venus in 1962.

- Major discoveries

  ⌐ Venus has a slow _____ _____ rate and high surface pressure and
    temperature.
  ├ Venus does not have a(n) _____ _____.
  └ Cosmic dust density levels are low.

② The Venera missions (Soviet Union)

  ⌐ In 1970, Venera 7 landed on the _____ of Venus.
  └ In 1975, Venera 9 and 10 became the first spacecraft to _____ Venus.

- Major discoveries

  ⌐ Venera 7 reported a surface temperature of _____ and a surface pressure of
    90 bar.
  └ Venera 9 and 10 took images showing a surface of sharp _____ and fine dust.

③ The Pioneer Venus missions (U.S.)

— In 1978, Pioneer Venus 1 and 2 orbited Venus.

- Major discoveries

  ⌐ A(n) _____ map of the surface of Venus was produced.
  └ Venus has enormous mountains and deep basins.

④ The Magellan mission (U.S.)

— In 1990, Magellan orbited Venus.

- Major discoveries

  — Venus has millions of _____ scattered randomly.

Vocabulary Review

A **Fill in the blanks with the best answer. Change the form if necessary.**

improvisation	regulate	striking	variability	incise	hemisphere

1. _____ as a form of musical expression is very significant in jazz.
2. They _____ their initials on the inside of their wedding rings.
3. _____ of weather cannot be underestimated when it comes to travel safety.
4. Air-conditioning and heating systems can be used to _____ room temperature.
5. People whose right _____ is more active are probably more creative and emotional than analytical and logical.

B **Choose the word or phrase that is closest in meaning to each highlighted word.**

1. The discussion topics prepared by the instructor were novel and refreshing.
   Ⓐ theoretical   Ⓑ debatable   Ⓒ easy   Ⓓ original

2. Writers tend to litter their desks with books, pieces of paper, dirty dishes and cups.
   Ⓐ provide   Ⓑ give up   Ⓒ mess up   Ⓓ fill

3. In the American Southwest, earthly-hued paintings with interesting patterns are common.
   Ⓐ colored   Ⓑ shaped   Ⓒ scented   Ⓓ oriented

4. Patience is a character trait that most people desire but find difficult to cultivate.
   Ⓐ advantage   Ⓑ superiority   Ⓒ attraction   Ⓓ attribute

5. Dinosaurs with feathers seem to have walked the earth in prehistoric times.
   Ⓐ golden   Ⓑ ancient   Ⓒ chaotic   Ⓓ given

6. Jane Austen always used the English countryside as the backdrop of her novels.
   Ⓐ climax   Ⓑ setting   Ⓒ plot   Ⓓ character

7. As he slept, incoherent speech came from his throat and he moved his arms wildly.
   Ⓐ speedy   Ⓑ angry   Ⓒ unintelligible   Ⓓ loud

C **Choose the correct word in each sentence.**

1. The laws of (perspective, precipitation) do not apply to various forms of modern art.
2. Listening to music too loudly through earphones can (imply, impair) one's hearing.
3. The company will (launch / launder) an experimental rocket in a few years.

Practice TOEFL iBT
Reading Section

Reading Section Directions

The Reading section measures your ability to understand academic passages in English.

Most questions are worth one point, but the last question in each set is worth more than one point. The directions indicate how many points you may receive.

Within each part, you can go to the next question by selecting **Next**. You can skip questions and go back to them later. If you want to return to previous questions, select **Back**. You can select **Review** at any time and the review screen will show you which questions you have answered and which you have not answered. From this review screen, you can go directly to any question you have already seen in the Reading section.

You may now begin the Reading section. In this part you will read 3 passages. You will have 54 minutes to read the passages and answer the questions.

Click **Continue** to go on.

Practice **TOEFL iBT**

The History of PCBs in the United States

→ Polychlorinated biphenyls (PCBs) have been used in electrical equipment because they can tolerate high temperatures and are efficient insulators. Scentless, tasteless, and colorless to pale yellow in color, PCBs may exist in solid, liquid, or gaseous states. Chemically, they are mixtures of up to 209 individual compounds. They do not have any known natural source.

→ First synthesized in 1881, PCBs were commercially manufactured in the United States   5
by the Swann Chemical Company in Anniston, Alabama, in 1927. By 1933, the company's employees were experiencing health problems related to PCB exposure. In addition to symptoms like appetite loss and lack of energy, employees developed rashes on their faces and bodies. Yet, in spite of the conspicuous link between employees' health issues and PCB exposure, use of the chemicals became more widespread. In 1935, the Swann Chemical Company was purchased by   10
the Missouri-based Monsanto Industrial Chemical Company, which licensed others to produce PCBs. Evidence in the form of a company memo indicates that during this very same year, Monsanto was unquestionably aware that PCBs were dangerous to humans. The memo noted that PCBs "cannot be considered nontoxic."

→ By the 1930s, it was becoming clear to the scientific community that PCBs were fairly   15
harmful. A 1937 Harvard study concluded that liver damage and a skin irritation called chloracne could result from prolonged exposure to PCBs. Studies conducted since then have demonstrated that PCBs cause a variety of cancers in lab animals and have resulted in the Environmental Protection Agency classifying them as a probable human carcinogen. ■ Since it would be unethical to intentionally expose humans to PCBs in order to test their toxicity, scientists cannot   20
use experiments to confirm that PCBs cause cancer in humans. ■ Yet, even limited studies indicate that it is quite likely that PCBs are indeed a human carcinogen. ■ In addition, it has been discovered that PCBs have other effects on human health. ■ For example, women exposed to PCBs during pregnancy may give birth to children with lower birth weights and significant motor control and neurological problems. Other research indicates that children exposed to PCBs   25
are more susceptible to diseases. Overall, the negative impact of PCBs on humans includes problems with the immune system, hormone system, reproductive system, and nervous system.

→ Human exposure to PCBs unfortunately often occurs as a result of environmental contamination. There are many tragic examples of the damage caused by the unregulated use and release of these chemicals into the environment. One of the most flagrant cases of PCB   30
dumping occurred at the hands of General Electric, which between 1947 and 1977 released 1.3 million pounds of PCBs into the Hudson River. GE claimed that the chemicals were safely buried in the Hudson River by clean sediment and that no cleanup was necessary because the PCBs would break down on their own. However, this position was simply not scientifically sound.

→ Over time, the sustained efforts of environmental advocates helped force GE into 35 accountability for its actions and brought about legislation to protect humans and the environment from the dangers of PCBs. As a result, in 1975 New York successfully sued GE to prevent the company from dumping PCBs into the Hudson, and by 1979 the U.S. Environmental Protection Agency had banned PCBs altogether. In 2009, GE finally began to dredge PCB-contaminated sediment along a forty-mile stretch of the Upper Hudson River. The company removed over 40 300,000 pounds of PCBs from the river, which was more than twice as much as the target amount, and completed the project in 2015. After thorough sediment sample testing, the EPA eventually announced that the company had achieved its goals in 2019.

1. The word tolerate in the passage is closest in meaning to

    (A) cool   (B) withstand   (C) produce   (D) regulate

2. The author states in paragraph 1 that PCBs

    (A) cannot be seen by the human eye   (B) are most useful as a liquid
    (C) do not occur in nature   (D) are divided into 209 types
    Paragraph 1 is marked with an arrow [→].

3. The word conspicuous in the passage is closest in meaning to

    (A) suspicious   (B) important   (C) unhealthy   (D) obvious

4. In paragraph 2, why does the author mention a Monsanto memo?

    (A) To indicate that Monsanto knew PCBs were dangerous as early as 1935
    (B) To explain how other companies received licenses to produce PCBs
    (C) To give an example of some of the undesirable effects of PCBs
    (D) To contrast the management of Monsanto with that of its predecessor
    Paragraph 2 is marked with an arrow [→].

PRACTICE TOEFL iBT

5. According to paragraph 3, PCBs are not classified as a confirmed human carcinogen because
   - A) studies of lab animals suggest that PCBs would not cause cancer in humans
   - B) scientists cannot specifically test whether PCBs cause cancer in humans
   - C) people who have been exposed to PCBs do not develop cancer
   - D) there have never been any studies of people exposed to PCBs

   Paragraph 3 is marked with an arrow [➡].

6. All of the following are mentioned in paragraph 3 as health problems caused by PCBs EXCEPT
   - A) increased risk of disease
   - B) reproductive disorders
   - C) skin irritations
   - D) loss of vision

   Paragraph 3 is marked with an arrow [➡].

7. Which of the sentences below best expresses the essential information in the highlighted sentence in the passage? *Incorrect* choices change the meaning in important ways or leave out essential information.
   - A) Because of environmentalists' work, GE was held responsible for what it had done and laws were created to limit PCBs' potential for harm.
   - B) When GE became accountable for its actions, laws could be put in place to protect people and the environment from further damage from PCBs.
   - C) Environmentalists' concern about the damaging effects of PCBs resulted in the development of laws to limit their use by GE.
   - D) Due to new laws prohibiting the release of PCBs into the environment, opponents of GE were able to hold the company accountable for the damage it had done.

8. Why does the author discuss General Electric in paragraphs 4 and 5?
   - A) To suggest that bans against PCB use were timely and effective
   - B) To give an example of a company that has tried to clean up the PCBs it produced
   - C) To demonstrate that PCBs were used across many industries
   - D) To introduce a particularly devastating example of unregulated PCB dumping

   Paragraphs 4 and 5 are marked with arrows [➡].

9. Look at the four squares [■] that indicate where the following sentence could be added to the passage.

    Instead, they must rely on studies of people who have been exposed to PCBs incidentally.

    Where would the sentence best fit?

    Click on a square [■] to add the sentence to the passage.

10. **Directions:** An introductory sentence for a brief summary of the passage is provided below. Complete the summary by selecting the THREE answer choices that express the most important ideas in the passage. Some sentences do not belong in the summary because they express ideas that are not presented in the passage or are minor ideas in the passage. *This question is worth 2 points.*

    > PCBs were used in America long after they were known to be harmful and have had a lasting impact on human and environmental health.
    >
    > •
    >
    > •
    >
    > •

    Answer Choices

    Ⓐ PCBs are chemicals that are extremely versatile and can exist in gaseous, liquid, and solid forms.

    Ⓑ Soon after PCBs were first manufactured in the U.S., it became clear to companies and scientists alike that PCBs were dangerous chemicals.

    Ⓒ When a 1937 Harvard study revealed that chloracne was caused by PCBs, the Environmental Protection Agency considered banning the chemicals.

    Ⓓ Though studies on humans are necessarily limited, PCBs have been proven to cause a number of serious health conditions.

    Ⓔ Human exposure to PCBs frequently occurs through direct contact with chemicals in the workplace.

    Ⓕ PCB dumping by General Electric helped spur activists and legislators to ban the chemicals and get the company to address the harm it had caused.

    Drag your answer choices to the spaces where they belong. To remove an answer choice, click on it. To review the passage, click on **View Text**.

Art Nouveau and Art Deco

Art Nouveau and Art Deco are two famous artistic movements that have influenced a wide variety of art forms. They were mostly the product of artists who wanted to create unique styles that represented the time and society they were a part of.

→ Art Nouveau, or *new art*, originated in England, became popular in Europe in the late 1800s, and reached the height of its popularity in the early 1900s. The goal of artists in favor ⁵ of this artistic movement, who ranged from architects and interior designers to illustrators and decorative artists, was to fuse both decorative and fine arts into a new form of art for the twentieth century. And in a period when mass-produced objects became the norm in society, these artists sought to return to their roots by honoring old-fashioned handmade craftsmanship that emphasized natural processes. Art Nouveau integrates organic shapes and natural elements, ¹⁰ such as plant stems, floral patterns, and insects. And even though it utilizes geometric shapes, the edges tend to be rounded and curved instead of hard and rigid. Its architects and artists favored long lines which bend and curve around on themselves, and they considered color secondary: natural greens and browns were most commonly employed, along with materials that blended in well with nature, like wood, iron, and glass. ¹⁵

→ Art Nouveau was the creation of the nineteenth-century Arts and Crafts movement, which favored making works by hand and the style of which was embodied in the works of textile designer William Morris. But it was Scottish architect Charles Rennie Mackintosh that created the idea that an object's style should not be predetermined but developed organically and that structures be based on function. Focusing on building from the inside out, he created his most ²⁰ famous building, the Glasgow School of Art, in 1910. Likewise, Catalan architect Antoni Gaudí employed his own unique style of design, best represented by his well-known works in Barcelona. Visual artists such as Austrian painter Gustav Klimt and Czech artist Alphonse Mucha also utilized Mackintosh's ideas in their abstract paintings of people. However, as World War I came to a close, Art Nouveau disappeared as new styles such as Art Deco began to replace it. ²⁵

→ In 1925, the International Exhibition of Decorative Arts and Modern Industries in Paris introduced the world to Art Deco. In fact, it was from this event that the term Art Deco originated from. The art itself was developed throughout the 1920s. It was mostly inspired by new manufacturing technology and utilized industrial materials, such as stainless steel, varieties of plastic, aluminum, and chrome. Rather than mimicking nature, Art Deco utilizes angular and ³⁰ geometric designs to create objects that appear smooth and futuristic. Vertical and rectilinear

Glossary

rectilinear: moving in or characterized by straight lines

designs are frequently used, such as upside down *V*s and zigzags, and structures often employed a variety of bold colors. Skyscrapers became some of the earliest and most memorable objects that followed this style.

The most iconic of these Art Deco skyscrapers was developed by architect William Van Alen 35 in 1928 with his easily recognizable Chrysler Building, a skyscraper made from stainless steel that honored technological progress. The art style also became common among decorative objects, such as furniture, jewelry, and glassworks. It could even be seen in the visual arts and sculpture. Certain visual artists employed the style in their print advertising and murals, while others used it in their portraits of illustrious figures. ■ Imposing monuments and sculptures that often weighed 40 hundreds of tons flourished in public spaces. ■ But after the stock market crash of 1929, people's focus turned toward mass production. ■ A simplified version of Art Deco known as Streamline Moderne appeared in the 1930s, which led to more one-story buildings for basic service needs. ■ Both Art Deco and Art Nouveau became less popular by World War II, however, as Modernism became the new artistic norm. 45

11. The word integrates in the passage is closest in meaning to
   Ⓐ follows   Ⓑ combines   Ⓒ accepts   Ⓓ reflects

12. The word embodied in the passage is closest in meaning to
   Ⓐ reviewed   Ⓑ expressed   Ⓒ undermined   Ⓓ influenced

13. The word it in the passage refers to
   Ⓐ a new style   Ⓑ World War I   Ⓒ Art Nouveau   Ⓓ Art Deco

14. According to paragraph 3, what is true about Charles Rennie Mackintosh?
   Ⓐ He was opposed to the idea that an object's design should not be planned out.
   Ⓑ He argued that objects should be crafted organically, starting from the inside.
   Ⓒ He regarded form and aesthetic quality more important than function.
   Ⓓ He collaborated with Antoni Gaudí to construct the Glasgow School of Art.
   Paragraph 3 is marked with an arrow [➡].

PRACTICE TOEFL iBT

203

15. What can be inferred from paragraphs 2 and 3 about the Art Nouveau movement?

     (A) It promoted using environmentally friendly materials.

     (B) It was founded by textile designer William Morris.

     (C) It was a reaction to mass production in society.

     (D) It replaced Art Deco at the end of World War I.

    Paragraphs 2 and 3 are marked with arrows [➡].

16. Which of the sentences below best expresses the essential information in the highlighted sentence in the passage? *Incorrect* choices change the meaning in important ways or leave out essential information.

     (A) Art Deco objects looked more modern and futuristic since they were influenced by both nature and geometry.

     (B) Unlike nature, which is complex, Art Deco relied on simple geometric shapes that could be easily replicated by other artists.

     (C) By mirroring the smooth lines of nature, Art Deco artists were able to design objects that were practical.

     (D) Favoring geometric designs that gave objects a futuristic look, Art Deco artists chose not to copy nature.

17. According to paragraph 4, all of the following are mentioned as characteristics of Art Deco EXCEPT

     (A) use of industrial materials

     (B) promotion of organic shapes

     (C) utilization of vivid colors

     (D) use of vertical designs

    Paragraph 4 is marked with an arrow [➡].

18. Why does the author mention the stock market crash of 1929?

     (A) To describe why an art form became less popular

     (B) To stress the great value of mass production

     (C) To explain the demand for more public artwork

     (D) To show how the economy heavily affects art galleries

REVIEW ✔   HELP ?   BACK ◀   NEXT ▶

19. Look at the four squares [■] that indicate where the following sentence could be added to the passage.

> Being an expensive artistic style to produce, Art Deco was mostly enjoyed by the affluent.

Where would the sentence best fit?

Click on a square [■] to add the sentence to the passage.

20. **Directions:** Complete the table by matching the statements below. Select the appropriate statements from the answer choices and match them to the type of art movement to which they relate. TWO of the answer choices will NOT be used. **This question is worth 3 points.**

Drag your answer choices to the spaces where they belong. To remove an answer choice, click on it. To review the passage, click on **View Text**.

Answer Choices	Art Nouveau
Ⓐ It utilizes natural elements and organic shapes. ▶	
Ⓑ Its most well-known structure is probably the Chrysler Building. ▶	
Ⓒ It originated from the Arts and Crafts movement.	**Art Deco**
Ⓓ It tries to show realistic images of people and the world. ▶	
Ⓔ It is known for its smooth and angular designs. ▶	
Ⓕ It was first made popular by American immigrants. ▶	
Ⓖ Its name originated from an exposition held in Paris.	

The Continental Drift Theory

➡ The theory stating that continents move slowly across the earth's surface, changing their positions relative to one another, is known as continental drift. It was proposed by Francis Bacon and others as early as 1600, based on the observation that the shorelines of the continents roughly fit together like the pieces of a giant puzzle. However, this theory was not widely accepted, since most geologists of the time believed that continents and oceans were ⁵ permanent, unchanging fixtures on the face of the planet.

➡ In 1912, Alfred Wegener, a multidisciplinary German scientist with an interest in geophysics, presented his own continental drift theory. Wegener proposed that a single great landmass he called Pangaea had once existed. This supercontinent was then separated into two by an ocean, with Laurasia to the north and Gondwanaland occupying the south. He ¹⁰ hypothesized that the breakup of Pangaea began approximately 200 million years ago, as the modern continents gradually separated and began to drift away from one another. It was not until about 70 million years ago, according to his theory, that the landmasses of the earth more or less assumed their modern configuration.

Wegener developed his hypothesis while researching the fossils of certain ferns and reptiles, ¹⁵ hundreds of millions of years old, which had been discovered on several different continents. ■ It was puzzling to scientists of the time as to how a single species of plant or animal would have been able to cross distances as vast as the oceans that separated the continents. ■ Wegener concluded that this mystery could be logically explained by the concept of Pangaea. ■ He pointed out that, along with their shorelines, other geophysical features of the continents such as ²⁰ mountain ranges matched up when Pangaea was hypothetically reassembled. ■ Wegener further noted that evidence of major climate changes in some of the continents, such as fossils of tropical plant species found in the frozen wasteland of Antarctica, could be attributed to continental drift, indicating that landmasses had occupied very different global positions in the past.

➡ The geological community quickly entered into strenuous debate over Wegener's theory ²⁵ of continental drift. Its opponents argued that not only was the fit of the continental shorelines vague and uneven, but these shorelines would have eroded significantly over the hundreds of millions of years since Pangaea had supposedly broken up, leaving them vastly altered. More importantly, the bulk of the scientific community flatly refused to believe that masses of land as large as the continents could move. In fact, Wegener was unable to develop a credible scientific ³⁰ explanation of the forces behind this theorized travel of the continents. He suggested that the continents moved by grinding their way through the earth's crust, powered by tides and the centrifugal force of the spinning planet. However, most scientists held that it would be physically impossible for a large mass of solid rock to remain intact while cutting through the ocean floor.

→ As scientists attempted to address the shortcomings of Wegener's theory, a new, more ³⁵ comprehensive idea was born: the theory of plate tectonics. It proposed that the earth's surface is broken up into six large plates and many smaller ones, all of which move about by floating atop a layer of extremely hot, soft rock known as the asthenosphere. As geologists of the 1960s began to acknowledge the undeniable truth of plate tectonics, Wegener's continental drift theory was brought back into the light of scrutiny. Eventually, after recognizing plate tectonics as the ⁴⁰ force that powered their movement, the theory of drifting continents was accepted by most geophysicists as scientific fact. Unfortunately for Wegener, he had died many years earlier and never had the chance to experience the accolades of his peers.

21. What can be inferred from paragraph 1 about Francis Bacon's theory about continental drift?
    (A) It represented mainstream scientific belief.
    (B) It did not offer any scientific proof.
    (C) It was similar to earlier theories on the issue.
    (D) It was accepted only by geologists.
    Paragraph 1 is marked with an arrow [→].

22. Why does the author discuss Pangaea in paragraph 2?
    (A) To describe a fundamental aspect of Wegener's theory
    (B) To explain the origins of Laurasia and Gondwanaland
    (C) To give details of Wegener's background in geophysics
    (D) To illustrate support for the theory of continental drift
    Paragraph 2 is marked with an arrow [→].

23. Which of the sentences below best expresses the essential information in the highlighted sentence in the passage? *Incorrect* choices change the meaning in important ways or leave out essential information.
    (A) The existence of tropical fossils in Antarctica was also used by Wegener to suggest the movement of continents around the globe.
    (B) While Wegener was researching his theory of continental drift, he was puzzled by the discovery of tropical plant fossils in the cold environment of Antarctica.
    (C) According to Wegener, if the earth's landmasses had indeed drifted beyond their current positions, that would explain the strange locations of tropical fossils.
    (D) Wegener's theory of continental drift was unable to account for the presence of foreign fossils buried in Antarctica.

24. The word strenuous in the passage is closest in meaning to

   Ⓐ public   Ⓑ intense   Ⓒ ongoing   Ⓓ in-depth

25. The word them in the passage refers to

   Ⓐ opponents   Ⓑ shorelines   Ⓒ masses of land   Ⓓ continents

26. According to paragraph 4, why did Wegener's opponents dismiss the observation that continental shorelines might have once fit together?

   Ⓐ Because the shorelines would have most likely eroded significantly over time

   Ⓑ Because the geological features of the continents do not match

   Ⓒ Because most species are too different to have come from a shared landmass

   Ⓓ Because not all the continents have coastlines that match

   Paragraph 4 is marked with an arrow [➡].

27. The word accolades in the passage is closest in meaning to

   Ⓐ answers   Ⓑ praises   Ⓒ criticisms   Ⓓ opinions

28. In paragraph 5, the author states that the theory of plate tectonics improved on the theory of continental drift by

   Ⓐ explaining how continents are able to shift positions

   Ⓑ providing more accurate data on the asthenosphere

   Ⓒ scientifically proving all the concepts in Wegener's theory

   Ⓓ revising the description of the earth's continental plates

   Paragraph 5 is marked with an arrow [➡].

29. Look at the four squares [■] that indicate where the following sentence could be added to the passage.

   A similar correlation in the types of rock found in Africa and South America, as well as the glacial debris in various locations around the world, also supported the notion of continental drift.

   Where would the sentence best fit?

   Click on a square [■] to add the sentence to the passage.

30. **Directions:** An introductory sentence for a brief summary of the passage is provided below. Complete the summary by selecting the THREE answer choices that express the most important ideas in the passage. Some sentences do not belong in the summary because they express ideas that are not presented in the passage or are minor ideas in the passage. *This question is worth 2 points.*

> Though the concept of continental drift had been proposed before, it was Alfred Wegener who is credited with formulating the groundbreaking theory.
>
> •
>
> •
>
> •

Answer Choices

(A) An important element of Wegener's hypothesis was the existence of a historical supercontinent known as Pangaea.

(B) According to Wegener, it was not until 70 million years ago that the continents we know today took shape.

(C) Wegener used his ideas about Pangaea and continental drift to explain some of the major geological mysteries of the time.

(D) When the idea of continental drift was first proposed, most geologists believed that the continents were fixed.

(E) Insufficient explanation about the forces powering continental drift caused the theory to be dismissed, but the later discovery of plate tectonics ultimately proved it to be true.

(F) The notion of plate tectonics was based on Wegener's theory and suggested that a layer called the asthenosphere moved the continents.

> Drag your answer choices to the spaces where they belong. To remove an answer choice, click on it. To review the passage, click on **View Text**.

Answer Keys

UNIT 01 Vocabulary

VOCABULARY PREVIEW
p. 13

A 1. Ⓕ 2. Ⓓ 3. Ⓔ 4. Ⓐ 5. Ⓑ
B 1. Ⓕ 2. Ⓓ 3. Ⓑ 4. Ⓖ 5. Ⓐ 6. Ⓔ
C 1. Ⓐ 2. Ⓑ 3. Ⓐ 4. Ⓑ

BASIC DRILLS
p. 15

1. Ⓒ 2. Ⓒ 3. Ⓑ 4. Ⓑ 5. Ⓓ 6. Ⓐ

READING PRACTICE
pp. 16~19

01 1. Ⓑ 2. Ⓓ 3. Ⓑ
   Extra Question Ⓓ
   Organization
   wealth, social rank, reputation

02 1. Ⓑ 2. Ⓓ 3. Ⓑ
   Extra Question Ⓒ
   Summary
   plaster, Rome, interior decoration, houses, bigger

iBT PRACTICE
pp. 20~25

01 1. Ⓓ 2. Ⓒ 3. Ⓐ 4. Ⓐ 5. Ⓒ
   6. Ⓓ 7. Ⓒ, Ⓓ, Ⓔ
02 1. Ⓓ 2. Ⓒ 3. Ⓑ 4. Ⓐ 5. Ⓑ
   6. Ⓓ 7. Ⓐ, Ⓓ, Ⓕ

ACTUAL PRACTICE TEST
pp. 26~29

1. Ⓐ 2. Ⓑ 3. Ⓓ 4. Ⓒ 5. Ⓑ 6. Ⓑ
7. Ⓑ 8. Ⓓ 9. 4th 10. Ⓐ, Ⓔ, Ⓕ

ORGANIZATION
p. 30

sensory perceptions, environment, symbols, proficient, perspective, abstract, several features, abstract concepts, modern psychology, education

VOCABULARY REVIEW
p. 31

A 1. manifest 2. diminish 3. feature 4. retain
   5. gross
B 1. Ⓓ 2. Ⓒ 3. Ⓒ 4. Ⓐ 5. Ⓑ
   6. Ⓐ 7. Ⓑ
C 1. popularize 2. personify 3. incompatible

UNIT 02 Reference

VOCABULARY PREVIEW
p. 33

A 1. Ⓓ 2. Ⓑ 3. Ⓐ 4. Ⓒ 5. Ⓕ
B 1. Ⓓ 2. Ⓐ 3. Ⓒ 4. Ⓑ 5. Ⓔ 6. Ⓕ
C 1. Ⓑ 2. Ⓑ 3. Ⓐ 4. Ⓑ 5. Ⓑ

BASIC DRILLS
p. 35

1. Ⓐ 2. Ⓓ 3. Ⓐ 4. Ⓑ

Vocabulary
1. Ⓓ 2. Ⓒ 3. Ⓑ 4. Ⓓ

READING PRACTICE
pp. 36~39

01 1. Ⓐ 2. Ⓑ 3. Ⓒ
   Extra Question Ⓑ
   Organization
   Deltas, triangular, evenly, irregular, Mississippi, branching channels, islands

02 1. (A)   2. (D)   3. (A)

Extra Question (A)

Summary

American Revolution, record keeping, middle class, Silhouette portraits, resemblance

iBT PRACTICE   pp. 40~45

01 1. (A)   2. (B)   3. (C)   4. (A)   5. (C)
    6. (B)   7. (B), (E), (F)

02 1. (A)   2. (C)   3. (B)   4. (D)   5. (C)
    6. 1st   7. (A), (B), (D)

ACTUAL PRACTICE TEST   pp. 46~49

1. (C)   2. (C)   3. (D)   4. (A)   5. (D)   6. (C)
7. (C)   8. (A)   9. 2nd   10. Mutualism: (B), (F) /
Parasitism: (C), (E) / Commensalism: (A)

ORGANIZATION   p. 50

association, Egyptian plovers, obligate, damaged, Endoparasite, benefits, Clownfish, Symbiosis

VOCABULARY REVIEW   p. 51

A 1. locomotive   2. profile   3. immoral
   4. gossip   5. hailed

B 1. (C)   2. (A)   3. (B)   4. (B)   5. (D)
   6. (A)   7. (D)

C 1. delta   2. viable   3. modesty

UNIT 03
Fact & Negative Fact

VOCABULARY PREVIEW   p. 53

A 1. (E)   2. (F)   3. (D)   4. (B)   5. (A)

B 1. (F)   2. (C)   3. (B)   4. (E)   5. (A)   6. (D)

C 1. (A)   2. (A)   3. (B)   4. (A)   5. (B)

BASIC DRILLS   p. 55

1. (C)   2. (D)

Vocabulary

1. (D)   2. (A)   3. (B)   4. (D)

READING PRACTICE   pp. 56~59

01 1. (A)   2. (D)   3. (D)

Summary

circumference, summer solstice, angles, Alexandria, 50 times

02 1. (D)   2. (C)   3. (A)

Organization

rain shower, cumulus cloud, precipitation, cold, lightning, 30 minutes

iBT PRACTICE   pp. 60~65

01 1. (B)   2. (D)   3. (D)   4. (A)   5. (C)
    6. (D)   7. (B), (E), (F)

02 1. (D)   2. (B)   3. (B)   4. (A)   5. (B)
    6. (C)   7. Johannes Dobereiner: (B), (D) /
John Newlands: (A), (G) / Dmitri Mendeleev:
(C), (E), (I)

ACTUAL PRACTICE TEST
pp. 66~69

1. D 2. A 3. C 4. C 5. D 6. A
7. A 8. B 9. 3rd 10. B , D , F

ORGANIZATION
p. 70

film projector, special effects, Theater Robert-Houdin, accident, jammed, double, slow

VOCABULARY REVIEW
p. 71

A 1. slanted 2. hock 3. vague 4. intact
   5. discard 6. manipulate
B 1. B 2. D 3. A 4. B 5. C
   6. C 7. D
C 1. projector 2. speculating 3. precipitation

UNIT
04 **Sentence Simplification**

VOCABULARY PREVIEW
p. 73

A 1. F 2. C 3. A 4. B 5. E
B 1. E 2. C 3. G 4. B 5. F 6. D
C 1. A 2. A 3. B 4. A 5. A

BASIC DRILLS
p. 75

1. D 2. D

READING PRACTICE
pp. 76~79

01 1. C 2. A
    Summary
    Neptune, diamonds, methane, pressure, carbon atoms

---

02 1. D 2. D
    Organization
    refraction, direction, white light, mirrors, lenses, clearer vision

iBT PRACTICE
pp. 80~85

01 1. B 2. B 3. D 4. D 5. C
    6. B 7. B , C , E
02 1. B 2. A 3. B 4. B 5. C
    6. D 7. C , D , F

ACTUAL PRACTICE TEST
pp. 86~89

1. A 2. B 3. C 4. C 5. B 6. D
7. B 8. D 9. 1st 10. B , E , F

ORGANIZATION
p. 90

modern American, central, economic, immigrants, blue-collar workers, middle class, modern

VOCABULARY REVIEW
p. 91

A 1. finalize 2. aid 3. Gloom 4. encircles
   5. reproducible
B 1. C 2. B 3. A 4. D 5. D
   6. C 7. B
C 1. forge 2. embrace 3. condense

UNIT 05 Inference

VOCABULARY PREVIEW
p. 95

A 1. Ⓔ 2. Ⓑ 3. Ⓐ 4. Ⓓ 5. Ⓒ
B 1. Ⓐ 2. Ⓓ 3. Ⓖ 4. Ⓔ 5. Ⓑ 6. Ⓕ
C 1. Ⓐ 2. Ⓑ 3. Ⓐ 4. Ⓐ 5. Ⓑ

BASIC DRILLS
p. 97

1. Ⓑ 2. Ⓐ

Vocabulary

1. Ⓒ 2. Ⓒ 3. Ⓐ

READING PRACTICE
pp. 98~101

01 1. Ⓐ 2. Ⓓ

Extra Question Ⓒ
Summary
classical tradition, perfection, antique art, nude, competitions, career

02 1. Ⓑ 2. Ⓓ

Extra Question Ⓐ
Summary
Shell middens, flood plains, bones, climatic, neutralize

iBT PRACTICE
pp. 102~107

01 1. Ⓒ 2. Ⓓ 3. Ⓐ 4. Ⓐ 5. Ⓒ
   6. Ⓒ 7. Ⓐ, Ⓒ, Ⓕ
02 1. Ⓐ 2. Ⓓ 3. Ⓐ 4. Ⓒ 5. Ⓒ
   6. Ⓑ 7. Ⓐ, Ⓑ, Ⓕ

ACTUAL PRACTICE TEST
pp. 108~111

1. Ⓐ 2. Ⓑ 3. Ⓒ 4. Ⓑ 5. Ⓑ 6. Ⓒ
7. Ⓐ 8. Ⓒ 9. 2nd 10. Ⓐ, Ⓒ, Ⓔ

ORGANIZATION
p. 112

Richard Nixon, Vietnam War, burglars, wiretap, won, Saturday Night Massacre, impeachment hearings, Supreme Court

VOCABULARY REVIEW
p. 113

A 1. aspiring 2. reversal 3. aesthetic
   4. legion 5. burglar
B 1. Ⓐ 2. Ⓐ 3. Ⓑ 4. Ⓓ 5. Ⓐ
   6. Ⓑ 7. Ⓒ
C 1. reign 2. malfunctioning 3. inherit

UNIT 06 Rhetorical Purpose

VOCABULARY PREVIEW
p. 115

A 1. Ⓒ 2. Ⓕ 3. Ⓑ 4. Ⓔ 5. Ⓐ
B 1. Ⓕ 2. Ⓐ 3. Ⓓ 4. Ⓖ 5. Ⓔ 6. Ⓒ
C 1. Ⓐ 2. Ⓑ 3. Ⓑ 4. Ⓐ 5. Ⓑ

BASIC DRILLS
p. 117

1. Ⓒ 2. Ⓐ

Vocabulary

1. Ⓑ 2. Ⓐ 3. Ⓒ

READING PRACTICE
pp. 118~121

01 1. Ⓐ 2. Ⓐ 3. Ⓒ

Summary
minerals, health, film, water softener, ion replacement

02 1. Ⓑ 2. Ⓒ 3. Ⓐ

Organization
water, New World, ocean, African fishermen

iBT PRACTICE
pp. 122~127

01 1. Ⓑ 2. Ⓓ 3. Ⓐ 4. Ⓐ 5. Ⓐ
   6. Ⓒ 7. Ⓒ, Ⓔ, Ⓕ
02 1. Ⓒ 2. Ⓓ 3. Ⓑ 4. Ⓓ 5. Ⓐ
   6. 3rd 7. Ⓑ, Ⓒ, Ⓓ

ACTUAL PRACTICE TEST
pp. 128~131

1. Ⓓ 2. Ⓒ 3. Ⓓ 4. Ⓐ 5. Ⓐ 6. Ⓐ
7. Ⓒ 8. Ⓐ 9. 4th 10. Thermal energy: Ⓒ,
Ⓖ, Ⓗ / Tidal energy: Ⓐ, Ⓘ / Wave energy:
Ⓓ, Ⓕ

ORGANIZATION
p. 132

thermal, waves, intermediate fluid, vapor, site,
Dam, construction, pressure, sea level, spin,
traditional

VOCABULARY REVIEW
p. 133

A 1. sufficiently 2. subside 3. botanists
   4. appliance(s) 5. reservoir
B 1. Ⓒ 2. Ⓑ 3. Ⓐ 4. Ⓓ 5. Ⓐ
   6. Ⓑ 7. Ⓓ
C 1. plow 2. disperse 3. receded

UNIT 07 Insertion

VOCABULARY PREVIEW
p. 137

A 1. Ⓒ 2. Ⓑ 3. Ⓕ 4. Ⓔ 5. Ⓓ
B 1. Ⓓ 2. Ⓐ 3. Ⓑ 4. Ⓖ 5. Ⓒ 6. Ⓕ
C 1. Ⓑ 2. Ⓑ 3. Ⓑ 4. Ⓑ 5. Ⓐ

BASIC DRILLS
p. 139

1. 2nd 2. 4th
Vocabulary
1. Ⓓ 2. Ⓐ 3. Ⓒ 4. Ⓐ

READING PRACTICE
pp. 140~143

01 1. 2nd 2. 1st
   Extra Question Ⓐ
   Summary
   ocean, octopuses, squids, ink

02 1. 4th 2. 2nd
   Extra Question Ⓓ
   Summary
   brain, cornea, lens, inverted, retina, optic nerve,
   sight

iBT PRACTICE
pp. 144~149

01 1. Ⓓ 2. Ⓓ 3. Ⓑ 4. Ⓓ 5. Ⓐ
   6. 3rd 7. Ⓐ, Ⓓ, Ⓔ
02 1. Ⓑ 2. Ⓓ 3. Ⓐ 4. Ⓑ 5. Ⓐ
   6. 3rd 7. Ⓐ, Ⓒ, Ⓔ

ACTUAL PRACTICE TEST
pp. 150~153

1. Ⓐ 2. Ⓐ 3. Ⓑ 4. Ⓓ 5. Ⓐ 6. Ⓓ
7. Ⓐ 8. Ⓓ 9. 3rd 10. Ⓐ, Ⓓ, Ⓔ

ORGANIZATION
p. 154

hand, China, carving, letter, quickly, price, Latin,
Renaissance

VOCABULARY REVIEW
p. 155

A 1. cast 2. angular 3. buds 4. impulse
   5. ledges

B 1. D   2. A   3. D   4. C   5. B
6. A   7. B
C 1. petals   2. barren   3. distinctions

UNIT 08 Prose Summary

VOCABULARY PREVIEW

A 1. A   2. C   3. D   4. E   5. F
B 1. A   2. G   3. C   4. B   5. F   6. D
C 1. B   2. B   3. B   4. A   5. A

BASIC DRILLS

p. 159

1. B, D, E

READING PRACTICE

pp. 160~163

01   1. A, C, D
02   1. B, D, E

iBT PRACTICE

pp. 164~169

01   1. C   2. B   3. B   4. D   5. A
6. A   7. B, E, F
02   1. C   2. D   3. B   4. A   5. D
6. D   7. A, D, E

ACTUAL PRACTICE TEST

pp. 170~173

1. C   2. D   3. B   4. C   5. B   6. C
7. D   8. C   9. 3rd   10. B, C, F

ORGANIZATION

p. 174

Charles Darwin, primeval soup, methane, electric current, amino acids, lightning storms, ancient atmosphere

VOCABULARY REVIEW

p. 175

A 1. amend   2. divine   3. devastation
4. archers   5. weathervane
B 1. B   2. C   3. D   4. A   5. C
6. A   7. B
C 1. commence   2. simulate   3. validity

UNIT 09 Schematic Table

VOCABULARY PREVIEW

p. 177

A 1. F   2. E   3. A   4. C   5. B
B 1. F   2. B   3. D   4. E   5. A   6. C
C 1. A   2. B   3. A   4. B   5. A

BASIC DRILLS

p. 179

1. Endotherm: A, B, F / Ectotherm: C, G

READING PRACTICE

pp. 180~183

01   1. Broca's area: B, C /
Wernicke's area: A, F, G
Extra Question   D

02   1. Black-figure style: A, D /
Red-figure style: C, F, G
Extra Question   B

iBT PRACTICE

01 1. Ⓐ   2. Ⓒ   3. Ⓐ   4. Ⓑ   5. Ⓓ
    6. Ⓑ   7. Ragtime: Ⓐ, Ⓕ, Ⓖ / Blues:
    Ⓒ, Ⓔ
02 1. Ⓒ   2. Ⓐ   3. Ⓐ   4. Ⓒ   5. Ⓒ
    6. Ⓒ   7. Binary fission: Ⓓ, Ⓖ / Budding:
    Ⓐ, Ⓒ / Fragmentation: Ⓑ

ACTUAL PRACTICE TEST
pp. 190~193

1. Ⓒ   2. Ⓓ   3. Ⓐ   4. Ⓓ   5. Ⓒ   6. Ⓓ
7. Ⓐ   8. Ⓑ   9. 1st   10. Findings of U.S.
spacecrafts: Ⓑ, Ⓓ, Ⓔ, Ⓘ / Findings of
Soviet spacecrafts: Ⓐ, Ⓖ, Ⓗ

ORGANIZATION
p. 194

retrograde rotation, magnetic field, surface, orbit,
475°C, rocks, topographical, volcanoes

VOCABULARY REVIEW
p. 195

A 1. Improvisation   2. incised   3. Variability
   4. regulate   5. hemisphere
B 1. Ⓓ   2. Ⓒ   3. Ⓐ   4. Ⓓ   5. Ⓑ   6. Ⓑ
   7. Ⓒ
C 1. perspective   2. impair   3. launch

Practice TOEFL iBT Reading Section
pp. 198~209

1. Ⓑ   2. Ⓒ   3. Ⓓ   4. Ⓐ   5. Ⓑ   6. Ⓓ
7. Ⓐ   8. Ⓓ   9. 2nd   10. Ⓑ, Ⓓ, Ⓕ
11. Ⓑ   12. Ⓑ   13. Ⓒ   14. Ⓑ   15. Ⓒ
16. Ⓓ   17. Ⓑ   18. Ⓐ   19. 2nd
20. Art Nouveau: Ⓐ, Ⓒ / Art Deco: Ⓑ, Ⓔ,
Ⓖ   21. Ⓑ   22. Ⓐ   23. Ⓐ   24. Ⓑ
25. Ⓑ   26. Ⓐ   27. Ⓑ   28. Ⓐ   29. 4th
30. Ⓐ, Ⓒ, Ⓔ